THREE ROADS BACK

Three Roads Back

HOW EMERSON, THOREAU, AND
WILLIAM JAMES RESPONDED TO
THE GREATEST LOSSES OF
THEIR LIVES

ROBERT D. RICHARDSON

WITH A FOREWORD BY
MEGAN MARSHALL

PRINCETON UNIVERSITY PRESS
PRINCETON & OXFORD

Published by Princeton University Press
41 William Street, Princeton, New Jersey 08540
99 Banbury Road, Oxford OX2 6JX

press.princeton.edu

All Rights Reserved

ISBN 9780691224305
ISBN (e-book) 9780691224312

British Library Cataloging-in-Publication Data is available

Editorial: Anne Savarese & James Collier
Production Editorial: Ali Parrington
Jacket Design: Jason Anscomb
Production: Erin Suydam
Publicity: Jodi Price & Carmen Jimenez
Copyeditor: Karen Verde

Jacket image: Look and Learn / Illustrated Papers Collection /
Bridgeman Images

This book has been composed in Arno

Printed on acid-free paper. ∞

Printed in the United States of America

10 9 8 7 6 5 4 3 2 1

CONTENTS

Foreword by Megan Marshall   ix

Preface   xvii

PART I. EMERSON   1

  1 Building His Own World   1

  2 I Will Be a Naturalist   11

  3 The Gallantry of the Private Heart   15

  4 The Green World   21

  5 Regeneration Through Nature   27

PART II. THOREAU   29

  6 The Cup that My Father Gives Me   29

7 I Had Hoped to Be Spared This   32

8 On Every Side Is Depth
   Unfathomable   35

9 Only Nature Has a Right to
   Grieve Perpetually   38

10 Death Is the Law of New Life   41

11 My Friend Is My Real Brother   48

12 Emerson Commissions a
    Book Review   51

13 Our Own Limits Transgressed   60

PART III. WILLIAM JAMES   65

14 The Death of Minny Temple   66

15 Minny and Henry   68

16 Minny and William   76

17 From Panic and Despair to the
    Acceptance of Free Will   84

18   The Self-Governing Resistance
     of the Ego to the World   90

     Postscript   96

               Notes   99
               Index   105

FOREWORD

"Loss has been much on my mind lately," my friend and mentor Bob Richardson wrote to me in July 2019. Bob knew about the death that spring of my life partner, and he offered to send me a manuscript he'd just completed—"about how RWE HDT and Wm. James dealt with bad losses," he summed up in biographer's shorthand. Bob hoped this short book, which he then called simply "Resilience," might bring consolation.

Of course I accepted his offer. Soon I was reading the most extraordinary book on the "work" of mourning I would come across during my season of grief—the book we now know as *Three Roads Back: How Emerson, Thoreau, and William James Responded to the Greatest Losses of Their Lives.*

I read that summer as if searching for the right recipe—how to do it. In Bob's book I found familiar prescriptions: travel, reading, nature, friendship, journal-keeping, letter-writing. Yet all of this was delivered with heightened impact through a method Bob calls "documentary biography," in words and scenes lifted straight from the past, as if the book were a documentary film. *Three Roads Back* puts readers in the presence of Bob's subjects. We are *with* Emerson in Paris when he tours the vast botanical collections of the Jardin des Plantes and realizes "the limits of the possible are enlarged"; *with* Thoreau as he looks out over the fields of Concord and discovers he is no longer "saddened because these particular flowers or grasses will wither—for their death is the law of new life"; *with* William James when he writes in his journal, "tragedy is at the heart of us, go to meet it, work it to our ends."

Bob's guiding hand was there too: this documentary has a narrator, a firm-voiced and sympathetic friend. "Think of them as fellow human beings," Bob instructs, and surely that's how he saw Emerson, Thoreau, and James after decades of immersion in the details of their lives and works as their biographer. He could deliver the particulars. Time, we're often told, is the best, perhaps the only, cure for a deeply felt loss. But how much time? Bob had tallied the divergent spans of months or years it took each of his subjects to return to his desk. This mattered to me. I was worried—would the fog ever lift, would I write again? I saw that all three of Bob's characters did, in their own time. I might too.

———

Reading *Three Roads Back* now, with three years' distance from my own "bad loss," I realize how much more there is in this small book than I could absorb at a time of need. Bob liked to quote his own mentor, Walter Jackson Bate, on the value of "linking ourselves" imaginatively with the great figures of the past, through biographical reading and writing. The practice, Bate wrote in *The Burden of the Past*, allows us to "become freer—freer to be ourselves, to be what we most want and value." These lines served as the epigraph to *Thoreau: A Life of the Mind*. Yet Bob was never in the self-help business, not even with *Three Roads Back*. I had read his manuscript for instruction, seeking a recipe, and I had missed Bob's point.

As much as any of his magisterial biographies, *Three Roads Back* is a consideration of how America's foundational thinkers arrived at their ideas. It just happens that death played a role in the process—and in the ideas themselves. Emerson, Thoreau, and James were young men when they lost a wife, a brother, a treasured cousin. They were at the dawn of their careers, scarcely cognizant of what might become their life's work. Although loss was a feature of most young lives in the American nineteenth century, a hard truth to which many were forced to adapt—Emerson lost both his father and an older brother by age eight, a younger sister three years later—these particular deaths, arriving to mingle with and dash our protagonists' fledgling hopes for the future, were both devastating and catalytic.

Through a combination of self-examination and confrontation with the facts of the outer world, Bob writes, each of the three ultimately achieved a view "of death as an inescapable part of living, and an acceptance that, at some level, there is no death." For Emerson and Thoreau, nature revealed that "the very process of decay is a life process." For James, the philosopher of the will, the realization was more profoundly internal: "Death sits at the heart of each one of us," he wrote, enabling us to gather the "resources" within ourselves to maintain "a true and courageous spirit."

These notions, achieved in bereavement, inspired the mature philosophy each one began to explore and expound in his writing from the moment of recovery.

"Genius is the activity that repairs the decay of things," Emerson wrote in his essay, "The Poet." A drive to repair the rent in the fabric of their lives—through which they had glimpsed the near fact of death—impelled all three. When Bob tells us, "Their examples of resilience count among their lasting contributions to modern life," he means two things: we can learn from their examples how to find our way back, and, what they gave us as they moved forward became American philosophy.

———

Bob wrote these words, this book, just a year before his own death in June 2020, at age eighty-six. He couldn't have known his fate, but if loss was much on his mind that year, perhaps it was because he was looking back on the course of his own life. Although he never wrote of it, Bob had in common with his subjects an experience of early loss—the death of a younger sibling, who happened to share the name of Thoreau's beloved brother, John. Like John Thoreau, John Richardson was a golden boy, popular and athletic, good-natured, cherished. Leukemia took him at age seventeen in a matter of weeks. Older brother Bob, a college student, had been assisting their father on a research trip in England when news of John's grim diagnosis reached them. His father flew back; Bob returned by Cunard liner with their luggage, arriving home shortly before his brother's death in a hospital operating room during a final surgery.

Is it any wonder Bob's first biography told the story of a writer who held his brother John in his arms as he died, convulsing, delirious, of lockjaw? We need not ask how and when Bob Richardson learned resilience. And we know what it allowed him to do: write the enduring biographical works that are his legacy.

Bob must also have had his family, his many friends, and his devoted readers in mind as he wrote *Three Roads Back* and looked ahead to the loss they would one day experience at his death. We may read the book now as a documentary biography of Bob's own life of the mind, grateful to be in the presence, once again, of his fierce intelligence and sympathetic spirit, and to join him in the vigorous embrace of life through the study of fellow human beings.

—*Megan Marshall*
May 2022

PREFACE

In dark times, from the personal to the global, one way I have found to fight back against what is going wrong is to re-examine the lives and works of figures from the past. I have spent many decades with Ralph Waldo Emerson, Henry David Thoreau, and William James. All faced disaster, loss, and defeat, and their examples of resilience count among their lasting contributions to modern life.

Emerson taught his readers self-reliance, which he understood to mean self-trust, not self-sufficiency. Thoreau taught his readers to look to Nature—to the green world—rather than to political party, country, family, or religion for guidance on how to live. William James taught us to look to actual human experience, case by case, rather than to dogma or theory, and showed us how truth is not an abstract or absolute quality, but a process. Experience—testing—either validates or invalidates our assumptions. Further, James says, attention and belief are the same thing. What you give your attention to is the key to what you believe. Whoever or whatever commands your attention also controls what you believe.

What all three of these writers and thinkers teach, through their lives as much as their writings, is resilience—that is, how to recover from losses, how to get back up after being knocked down, how to construct prosperity out of the wreckage of disaster. To take this in, we need not only to read what they wrote, but also to look at how they lived their lives. This is the biggest contribution of the biographical approach, which focuses our attention on how they lived their own lives as well as on the continuing value of what they wrote.

A Note on Method

Forget for a moment, if you can, the contributions Emerson, Thoreau, or William James made to knowledge and to literature. Think of them as fellow human beings, facing losses and troubles much like ours. The method I am trying to use for these stories—and they *are* stories—is not critical discourse, nor is it ordinary biographical narrative, but instead is what we might call documentary biography.[1] The idea is to let them tell their stories in their own words as much as possible, from their journal entries and letters.[2] Some of the material will be familiar to readers and scholars. But the documentary method is intended to facilitate a personal, even a sympathetic, connection— rather than a detached, critical, or judgmental connection—between the reader and the subject.

Part I

Emerson

1. Building His Own World

A man must do the work with that faculty he
has now. But that faculty is the accumulation of
past days. . . . No rival can rival backwards. What
you have learned and done, is safe and fruitful.
Work and learn in evil days, in insulted days, in
days of debt and depression and calamity. Fight
best in the shade of the cloud of arrows.

—EMERSON, JMN 10:41[1]

A Moving World Without a Sun

On February 8, 1831, Ellen Tucker Emerson, the
wife of a young Boston minister, died of tuberculosis at home at nine in the morning. She was just
nineteen. She had met her husband—who would

become a well-known writer, lecturer, and public figure—in Concord, New Hampshire, when she was sixteen and he was eight years older. Ellen was engaged at seventeen, married at eighteen, and now, a year and four months later, she was dead, and her young husband was devastated. His name was Ralph Waldo Emerson, known to friends and family as Waldo.

Five days after Ellen's death, this twenty-seven-year-old Unitarian minister turned to his journal and wrote:

Five days are wasted since Ellen went to heaven to see, to know, to worship, to love, to intercede . . . Reunite us, O thou father of our spirits. There is that which passes away and never returns. This miserable apathy, I know, may wear off. I almost fear when it will. Old duties will present themselves with no more repulsive face. I shall go again among my friends with a tranquil countenance. Again I shall be amused. I shall stoop again to little hopes and little fears and forget the graveyard. But will the dead be restored to me? Will the eye that was closed on Tuesday ever beam again in the fulness of love for me? Shall I ever again be able to connect the face of outward nature, the mists of the morn, the stars of eve, the flowers, and all poetry, with the heart and life of an enchanting friend? No. There is one birth, and one baptism, and one first love, and the affections cannot keep their youth any more than men.[2]

This is a beautifully written entry with a memorable conclusion. But note also Emerson's rapid movement of thought, from conventional Christian pieties to a mild but embarrassed self-loathing; from questioning the idea of an afterlife to a final, blunt acceptance of mortality, of "one birth, and one baptism, and one first love," with the clear conclusion that there is one life and when it is over, it is over.

The entire passage is not only a forthright expression of grief, but also a premonition of the process young Emerson would go through over the next year and a half. Ellen's death plunged him into a "miserable apathy" that did not, in fact, wear off quickly. He was somber and preoccupied with his loss, walking out from Boston to Roxbury to visit her grave every day.

He was, in his own words, "unstrung, debilitated by grief." In the days just after her death he imagined he could still hear her breathing, could see her dying. He called out to her, prayed to her as an intercessory saint. He wrote that his whole life was one of "unrepaired regret." Everything was colored by the "heaviness of the fact of death."

Ellen had wanted to be a poet, had called her dog "Byron," and surviving examples of her writing show real promise.

> So I, unless God's guiding love
> Had brought thee to me from above,
> Might now have lived but half an one,
> A moving world without a sun.[3]

In June 1831, five months after her death, Emerson—himself a would-be poet—composed what we can read as a response to Ellen's lines.

> The days pass over me
> And I am still the same
> The Aroma of my life is gone
> Like the flower with which it came.[4]

As empty as he felt, however, he still had his job to do, his pastoral duties to perform. These included preaching and acting as spiritual guide to others just when he most needed one himself.

He managed to carry on, exhibiting a physical and intellectual resilience. He undertook a series of sermons that re-examined parts of the Bible using the method of the new German Higher Criticism, which his older brother William had studied with the great theologian Johann Gottfried Eichhorn (1752–1827), and which Waldo was now eager to learn and apply. This new method studied biblical texts by comparing them with each other, in their original languages. In this method the Bible was not something to venerate and accept uncritically as the word of God, but a set of historical documents like any other documents produced by men.

Along with his biblical studies, the bereft young Emerson was reading ever more deeply in what was then called natural philosophy but which we know as science. He read Mary Somerville's *Mechanism of the Heavens* (1831), an abridged English translation of Pierre Simon Laplace's French masterpiece on celestial mechanics. Somerville was a major scientist in her own right, proposing from her own observations of irregularities in the orbit of Uranus that there might be a hitherto unknown planet nearby: she was correct, and her research contributed to the discovery of Neptune. Emerson also found inspiration in John Herschel's *Preliminary Discourse on the Study of Natural Philosophy* (1831), which he was reading on the last day of December of that year. An investigator into natural phenomena, Herschel wrote, "cannot help perceiving that the insight he is enabled to obtain into this internal sphere of thought and feeling is in reality the source of all his power." Herschel described the natural philosopher as "Accustomed to trace the operation of general causes, and the exemplification of general laws, in circumstances where the uninformed and uninquiring eye perceives neither novelty nor beauty, he walks in the midst of wonders."

We can guess at the state of mind of the young minister when, in January 1832, not long after reading Herschel, he made this short journal entry: "It is the worst part of a man, I sometimes think, that is the minister."[5]

Not quite two months later, Emerson walked out to Roxbury to Ellen's tomb as usual, but this trip was very different, because this time he opened the coffin and looked at the body of his young wife, who had died fourteen months earlier. He wrote down nothing—or nothing that has survived—of what he saw. He wrote once about the "vanishing volatile froth of the present," and he would later say, of Thomas Carlyle: "his imagination, finding no nutriment in any creation, avenged itself by celebrating the majestic beauty of the laws of decay."[6] What exactly met his eye that day cannot have been pleasant, but he had to see it for himself.

Two months later, in May, Emerson told his Boston congregation, "I regard it as the irresistible effect of the Copernican Astronomy to have made the theological scheme of Redemption absolutely incredible." "Irresistible" and "absolutely incredible" do not suggest tentative or exploratory notions. The sentence is rock solid. As he had to see Ellen's remains for himself, so he now realized and accepted that he had to think for himself as well.

The Lord's Supper

Seven short days after this bold declaration of independent thought, Emerson wrote a letter (now lost) resigning from his position as junior minister in Boston's Second Church. The move signaled his separation from the ministry as a calling, and from Unitarian Christianity. Just as he was drafting his letter of resignation—maybe the very same day—he noted in his journal, "I have some-times thought that in order to be a good minister it was necessary to leave the ministry."[7]

Emerson left formal, inherited, traditional Christianity in 1832 and never returned. But he did not want to walk away from the personal, the social, the human relations, the communion be-tween and among like-minded people of faith—his parishioners. Emerson might no longer be a proper Christian, but he still had, and would always have, a religious nature. We can see this clearly in the sermon he gave as his farewell to his church on September 9, 1832, when he was twenty-nine years old.

The sermon discussed the Lord's Supper, also known as Communion. Here is how Emerson presented his subject:

> In the history of the Church no subject has been more fruitful of controversy than the Lord's Supper. There never has been any una-nimity in the understanding of its nature, nor any uniformity in the celebrating it. . . . Having recently given particular attention to this sub-ject, I was led to the conclusion that Jesus did not intend to establish an institution for per-

petual observance when he ate the Passover with his disciples, and, further, to the opinion that it is not expedient to celebrate it as we do. Now observe the facts.

Emerson then laid out his argument, which looks at the subject critically rather than reverentially:

Two of the Evangelists, namely Matthew and John, were of the twelve disciples, and were present on that occasion. Neither of them drops the slightest intimation of any intention on the part of Jesus to set up anything permanent. John, especially, the beloved disciple, who has recorded with minuteness the conversation and the transactions of that memorable evening, has quite omitted such a notice. Neither does it appear to have come to the knowledge of Mark who, though not an eyewitness, relates the other facts. This material fact, that the occasion was to be remembered, is found in Luke alone, who was not present.

It is significant that Emerson chose the subject of Communion to make his break with the Church. What he is objecting to is Communion as a universal sacrament, something to be required of all

Christians forever, an action formally prescribed for all time. What he does not object to is communion with a small c, the bonds between people. No longer interested in the religion of people who lived many centuries ago, he very much wanted "a religion by revelation to *us* and not the history of theirs."

He would develop these ideas in his 1836 book, *Nature,* but in 1832 he was still carving out his position, still reacting against formal, inherited, dogmatic Christianity. In October 1832, he was making comments on Christianity that have a bit of the saltiness and pithiness of the best of Thomas Carlyle, whose work Emerson was reading at the time. In his journal, Emerson imagined a little dialogue.

"You must be humble because Christ says 'Be humble.'"

"But why must I obey Christ?"

"Because God sent him."

"But how do I know God sent him?"

"Because your own heart teaches the same thing he taught."

"Why then should I not go to my own heart first?"

On December 22, Emerson wrote a final letter to his church explaining his position: "To me, as one disciple, is the ministry of truth, as far as I can discern and declare it, committed, and I desire to live nowhere and no longer than that grace of God is imparted to me." In other words, he is now committed to the truth *as he sees it.* And we can see from the tortured syntax how Emerson struggles to reconcile his need to pursue the truth as he sees fit with his desire to keep his connection, his communion, with his congregation: "I rejoice to believe, my ceasing to exercise the pastoral office among you, does not make any real change in our spiritual relation to each other." Emerson's intellectual and theological break with the Church was now complete, however strongly he hoped to keep his ordinary human, social bonds with his fellow men and women. Three days later he left Boston and boarded a ship bound for Europe.

2. I Will Be a Naturalist

Emerson's physical condition at the end of December 1832 was so poor that Captain Ellis, of the brig *Jasper*, was reluctant to take him on board lest he not survive the voyage. But Emerson did go,

one of five passengers on a ship loaded with log-
wood, mahogany, tobacco, sugar, coffee, beeswax,
and cheese. The first week was stormy and miserable, the passengers all confined below deck, ex-
periencing "nausea, darkness, unrest, unclean-
ness, harpy appetite and harpy feeding," but the
next four weeks brought decent weather. Emerson enjoyed learning about sailing and naviga-
tion, and he registered newfound respect for experience as opposed to mere words. "The thing
set down in words is not (thereby) affirmed," he
wrote in his journal on January 6. "It must affirm
itself or no form of grammar and no verisimili-
tude can give it evidence." And with a new and
firm sense of conviction, he added, "This is a
maxim which holds to the core of the world."[8]

After five weeks at sea, the *Jasper* reached
Malta, a small archipelago just south of Sicily.
Now an independent country and part of the
European Union, in February 1833, when Emerson landed there, it was a British colony. Emerson stayed a week, then moved on, first to Sicily
and then to Naples. He spent most of March in
Rome and most of April in Florence. On May 7,
while he was still in Northern Italy, a letter from
his brother Charles caught up with him and

flooded him with recollections of what he had left behind:

> Today I heard by Charles's letter, of the death of Ellen's mother. Fast, fast the bonds dissolve that I was so glad to wear. She has been a most kind and exemplary mother, and how painfully disappointed! Happy now, and oh, what events and thoughts in which I should have deepest sympathy does this thin partition of flesh entirely hide! Does the heart in that world forget the heart that did beat with it in this? Do jealousies, do fears, does the observation of faults intervene? Dearest friends, I would be loved by all of you; dearest friend! We shall meet again.[9]

Emerson left Milan for Switzerland on June 11, then spent July in Paris, where he had a vocational epiphany. Pursuing his interest in science, he went to the Sorbonne to hear Louis-Jacques Thenard and Joseph-Louis Gay-Lussac lecture on chemistry. Then, on July 13, he visited the Jardin des Plantes, a major scientific center that aimed for completeness in botanical classification and much else. He was astounded at the ornithological collections, remarking, "I wish I had come only there," and he listed many of the birds there assembled—tiny hummingbirds, birds-of-paradise, black swans, peacocks, ibis, flamingos, toucans, and vultures. He found himself deeply moved:

> The fancy colored vests of these elegant beings made me as pensive as the hues and forms of a cabinet of shells formerly. It is a beautiful collection and makes the visitor as calm and genial as a bridegroom. The limits of the possible are enlarged.

This is not a man who uses words carelessly. The phrase "calm and genial as a bridegroom" seems to mark Emerson's recovery of a state that had vanished with Ellen's death, and it sounds as though the young Emerson is indeed finally—exuberantly—back among the living. Wandering in this Paris museum of natural history, with its vast and orderly collections of animals, plants, minerals, shells, insects, and more, he is struck by "the upheaving principle of life everywhere incipient in the very rock aping organized forms." In Emerson's moment of connection with the natural world in the Jardin des Plantes, the force of life entirely overpowers the feelings of loss and despair he had so recently plumbed. His admiration for the French collections bursts through again and again: "In the other rooms I saw amber containing perfect mosquitoes, grand blocks of quartz, native gold in all its forms of crystallization, threads, plates, crystals, dust and silver, black as from fire. Ah! Said I, this is philanthropy, wisdom, taste, to form a cabinet of natural history."[10] "I feel the centipede in me," he wrote, "cayman, carp, eagle and fox. I am moved by strange sympathies. I say continually, I will be a naturalist."[11]

3. The Gallantry of the Private Heart

By August 5, 1833, Emerson had left France and crossed the Channel to England, where he met the poet Samuel Taylor Coleridge, who spent much of their time together abusing Unitarianism. Later that same month, Emerson met Thomas Carlyle at his home, Craigenputtock (roughly translatable as Hawk Hill, puttocks being small hawks), in Scotland. The family home of Carlyle's wife, Jane Welsh, the estate is in the district of Dumfries, southwest of Edinburgh and just across the Solway Firth from the English Lake country.

When Emerson was working himself out of the ministry, he had read an article about a book of poetry, *Corn Law Rhymes*, in the *Edinburgh Review*. The name of the poet, Ebenezer Elliott, was not given, nor was the name of the reviewer, Thomas Carlyle, whose language is salty, brisk, unconventional. The piece Emerson read in early October 1832 begins with these fetching sentences:

> Smelfungus Redivivus, throwing down his critical assaying balance some years ago, and taking leave of the Belles-Lettres function, expressed himself in this abrupt way: The end having come, it is fit that we end. Poetry having ceased to be read, or published, or written, how can it continue to be reviewed?

The anonymous review goes on, arch, elevated, sardonic, and punchy:

> Strange as it may seem, it is nevertheless true, that here we have once more got sight of a Book calling itself Poetry, yet which actually is a kind of Book, and no empty pasteboard Case, and simulacrum or "ghost-defunct" of a Book, such as is too often palmed on the world, and handed over Booksellers' counters with a demand of real money for it, as if it too were a reality.[12]

Emerson had found out the author's name and whereabouts, and now, on August 26, 1833, he arrived at Craigenputtock. He wrote about the meeting as "a White day in my years. I found the youth I sought" (Emerson was now 30, Carlyle 38), "and good and wise and pleasant he seems to me." Jane Welsh Carlyle thought Emerson's visit was like that of "an angel" and the best thing that happened while the Carlyles lived there, before they moved to London in 1834.

On August 26, 1833, Thomas Carlyle and his American visitor talked and walked for hours on end. By August 28, Emerson had left Craigenputtock to meet William Wordsworth at his home in England's Lake District. Carlyle later wrote about Emerson to his friend John Stuart Mill that what he "loved in the man was his health, his unity with himself; all people and all things seemed to find their quite peaceable adjustment with him." Emerson had come a long way from the sickly ex-parson who had crept onto a ship in Boston eight months earlier.

Carlyle had a great deal to offer Emerson, and Emerson was now, finally, open enough to be able to take it all in. To begin with, there was friendship. They had hit it off immediately and would remain good friends and correspondents for the rest of their lives. Carlyle was old enough to teach Emerson things, but young enough for them to be, more or less, equals.

Carlyle's language had captured Emerson's interest before he knew who was writing the articles he so admired in the *Edinburgh Review*. And Carlyle's language was always full of energy, whether it was the enthusiasm of his younger days or the angry, mordant pessimism of his later work. Carlyle's prose was intelligent without being academic and pungent without coarseness.

Carlyle was the flag carrier of the new transcendentalism, and he praised—and imitated— the German philosopher Johann Gottlieb Fichte, who said, "There is a Divine Idea pervading the visible universe; which visible universe is indeed but a symbol and sensible manifestation." Carlyle believed in the essential unity of all things; he found the idea also in Schelling and in Hinduism. According to this line of thought, there is a fundamental unity, a basic similarity in all human experience, which is finally more important than the many obvious differences.

Carlyle and his writing also helped Emerson think through his own specific religious problem with new clarity. By September 8, 1833, Emerson was on the ship headed for home, setting down in his journal some of what he had figured out: "Carlyle deprecated the state of a man living in rebellion, as he termed it, with no worship, no reverence for anybody. Himself, he said, would worship anybody who should show him more truth."[13] Emerson goes on to signal that he is going "back to myself":

I believe that the error of religionists lies in this, that they do not know the extent, or the harmony or the depth of their moral nature: that they are clinging to little, positive, verbal, formal versions of the moral law, and very imperfect versions too, while the infinite laws, the laws of the Law, the great circling truths whose only adequate symbol is the material laws [physics, chemistry] the astronomy etc. are all unobserved and sneered at when spoke of, as frigid and insufficient.

Then he calls Calvinism and Unitarianism each "such an imperfect version of the moral law."[14]

Perhaps the greatest of Carlyle's gifts to the young American was his pessimism about the present age and its materialism and utilitarianism, together with his advocacy for the heroic individual spirit. Much later, in a chapter on literature in *English Traits*, Emerson will come back around to describe Carlyle in a passage astonishing for its depth and nuance:

> In the decomposition and asphyxia that followed all this materialism, Carlyle was driven by his disgust at the pettiness and the cant, into the preaching of Fate. In comparison with all this rottenness, any check, any cleansing, though by fire, seemed desirable and beautiful. He saw little difference in the gladiators or the "causes" for which they combatted; the one comfort was, that they were all going speedily into the abyss together. And his imagination, finding no nutriment in any creation, avenged itself by celebrating the majestic beauty of the laws of decay. The necessities of mental structure force all minds into a few categories, and where impatience of the tricks of men makes Nemesis amiable, and builds altars to the negative Deity, the inevitable recoil is the heroism or the gallantry of the private heart, which decks its immolation with glory, in the unequal combat of will against fate.[15]

The phrase "the majestic beauty of the laws of decay" is worth lingering over. Was Emerson thinking back to Ellen's coffin?

4. The Green World

The thirty-year-old Emerson who came ashore back in Boston on October 9, 1833, was a different person from the sickly wreck who had boarded the *Jasper* in that same port nine months earlier. The Emerson who returned had a new intellectual and philosophical focus, new beliefs, a new profession, a new subject to write on, and lots of energy and enthusiasm for it all. He was a tall man, standing six feet in his shoes. He had narrow, sloping shoulders and a long neck, and he carried himself erectly. His eyes were very blue, his hair dark brown. He wore loose-fitting clothes and struck some observers as looking like a prosperous farmer. He carried his money in an old wallet wrapped in twine.

Less than a month after returning to Boston, Emerson had arranged for and delivered his first lecture for a general audience, "The Uses of Natural History."

The piece is a clear departure from the scholarly, theological bible-centered analysis of the ministerial world. It is an unapologetic embrace of what we would now call the green world. Emerson gave his listeners a rapturous account of the Jardin des

Plantes as "a grammar of botany where the plants rise each in its class, its order, its genus. . . . Imagine," he told his audience, "how much more exciting and intelligent is this natural alphabet, this green and yellow and crimson dictionary, on which the sun shines and the winds blow."[16]

This first lecture of Emerson's new career points directly to his first and, for many readers, his greatest book, *Nature*, which he would publish just three years later, in 1836. "The Uses of Natural History" is a kind of exploratory flight, a first rough sketch. Gone is the preacherly woe of Ecclesiastes ("The eye is not filled with seeing nor the ear with hearing"). Instead, says this new Emerson, "the eye is filled with seeing"—seeing Nature, that is. And now Emerson rushes to list and discuss what he calls the uses of Natural History. He lists five main uses, which are as true now as they were at the time.

1. Health. Taking an interest in Nature pushes us toward an outdoor life.
2. Commodity. Nature is useful to farmers and to everybody. It is the source of many of the things we need.
3. Delight. Nature delights the mind: "It needs only to have the eye informed to

make everything we see, every plant, every spider, every moss, every patch of mould upon the bark of a tree, give us the idea of fitness."

4. Education. Nature has an educative, disciplining effect on the mind.

5. "It is the effect of science to explain man to himself. . . . The knowledge of all the facts of all the laws of Nature will give man his true place in the system of beings."

Emerson is also very interested in language, which fills its own chapter in *Nature*. Here, in the "Uses of Natural History," he talks about the "power of expression which belongs to external nature, or that correspondence of the outward world to the inner world of thought and emotions." He also talks about the "secret sympathy which connects men to all the animals, and to all the inanimate world around him." And it is here that he first says, "the whole of nature is a metaphor of the human mind."[17] He ends the lecture with this insistence on the connection between humans and the natural:

Nature is a language and every fact one learns is a new word; but it is not a language taken to pieces and dead in the dictionary. But the language put together into a most significant and universal sense. I wish to learn this language, not that I may know a new grammar, but that I may read the great book which is written in that tongue.[18]

Action Proportioned to Nature

With his new subject, his new profession, and his new energy, Emerson's life must have seemed recovered, fully restored from the previous depths. And it was, though more changes lay just ahead. In April 1834, Emerson was feeling an infusion of energy from his aunt, Mary Moody Emerson, from Carlyle, and from the memory of the "delicious day when I woke to a strain of highest melody" (the moment of revelation in the Jardin des Plantes). He moved that year from Boston to Concord, and in 1835 he would marry again, to Lydia Jackson of Plymouth, Massachusetts.

But on the first day of October 1834, his brother Edward died at age twenty-nine. In July 1835, Emerson's comments on Christianity in his journal have a real edge as he lists the defects of Jesus.

He wrote, "I do not see in him cheerfulness. I do not see the love of natural science. I see in him no kindness for art, I see in him nothing of Socrates, of La Place, of Shakespeare."

On May 9, 1836, Emerson's younger brother Charles died at age twenty-eight. But in September of the same year, Emerson published his first and arguably greatest book, *Nature*, and on October 30, his first child, Waldo, was born.

Nature is the full flowering of the seeds planted in "The Uses of Natural History." The opening paragraph is a gentle dismissal of Christianity as a revelation that might have been relevant to earlier generations, but asks innocently, if pointedly, "why should not we *also* enjoy an original relation to the universe? Why should not *we* have a poetry and philosophy of insight and not of tradition, and a religion by revelation to *us*, and not the history of theirs?" He invites his readers to regeneration and redemption not through Christianity, but through "action proportioned to nature." And in the closing and climactic paragraph of the book, Emerson urges his readers to undertake the construction operation he himself has just been through. In his case it was a re-construction.

Know then that the world exists for you. For you is the phenomenon perfect. What we are, that only can we see. All that Adam had, all that Caesar could, you have and can do. Adam called his house Heaven and earth; Caesar called his house Rome; you perhaps call yours a cobbler's trade; a hundred acres of ploughed land; or a scholar's garret. Yet line for line and point for point your dominion is as great as theirs, though without the fine names. Build therefore your own world.

This is powerful, often quoted, livable and testable stuff. The present age is as good as any other if we only know how to take advantage of it. But the closing paragraph of *Nature* doesn't end here, with the emphasis on the strong individual. Emerson insists on a vision not of heaven but of a saved and regenerated world of nature.

As when the summer comes from the south, the snow banks melt and the face of the earth becomes green before it, so shall the advancing spirit create its ornaments along its path and carry with it the beauty it visits and the song which enchants it; it shall draw beautiful faces, warm hearts, wise discourse and heroic acts, around its way, until evil is no more seen.

The vision of the centrality and all-encompassing quality of nature that came to Emerson most spectacularly in the Jardin des Plantes in Paris unites Emerson's earliest and latest works. It is the theme not only of "The Uses of Natural History" and *Nature*, but also of the last—unfinished—project Emerson undertook, the "Natural History of Intellect."

5. Regeneration Through Nature

Regeneration, not through Christ but through Nature, is the great theme of Emerson's life, and it came to him as a response to the death of his young wife Ellen. Emerson uses the language of redemption, regeneration, and revelation—terms for what we would now call resilience. We can see three major points at which the conventional young minister of Unitarian Christianity transformed himself into the apostle of Nature. First comes the opening of Ellen's coffin. No resurrection there, just visual evidence of decay and the finality of death. Next—and quickly—comes the flat statement about the absolute impossibility of the "scheme of redemption" (through Christ), for Emerson an inescapable intellectual conclusion. Third, after a pause, came the thunderstroke, the revelation in the Jardin des Plantes of the wonder and power and interconnectedness of Nature, a religion of Nature that would shape the rest of his life.

Part II

Thoreau

6. The Cup that My Father Gives Me

On the last day of December 1841, Henry Thoreau, then twenty-four years old, wrote a 450-word entry in his journal, starting with the observation that "Books of natural history make the most cheerful winter reading." He mentions Audubon, the Florida Keys, Labrador, and "the snow on the forks of the Missouri." For three paragraphs he insists on the "singular health" he finds in such reading. "In society you will not find health, but in nature," he writes. "I should like to keep some kind of natural history always by me as a sort of elixir, the reading of which would restore the tone of my system and secure me true and cheerful views of life."[1]

The next day, a Saturday, New Year's Day, 1842, dawned in Concord with clear skies, but turned cloudy and squally. It was a day like any other, except that Henry's brother John, three years older than Henry, cut himself on the ring finger of his left hand while shaving. He thought nothing of it, wrapped a bandage around the cut, and went on with life as usual.

Henry was working at his journal, as he usually did for a part of each day. He was reading Chaucer and liking it. A couple of days later, on Monday, January 3, he made popcorn, which he playfully called "cerealious blossoms" because they were "only a more rapid blossoming of the seed under a greater than July heat." On Wednesday, January 5, as early clouds gave way to midday sun, he praised manual labor as "the best method to remove palaver from one's style." Maybe he took his own advice about palaver. We hear no more from him about cerealious blossoms.

On Saturday, January 8, eight days after he'd cut himself, John found his cut "mortified," that is, gangrenous. He walked to the town doctor, Josiah Bartlett, who dressed the wound and sent him home. Leaving the doctor's house, John felt weak and barely made it home. The next morning, he felt his jaw muscles stiffening. By evening, lockjaw (tetanus) had set in. Henry became John's nurse, but John's condition deteriorated fast. The next day, Monday, January 10, a Boston doctor was sent for, came out to Concord, and pronounced the case hopeless. Hearing this, John is reported to have said, "The cup that my father gives me; shall I not drink it?"

John died the next day, Tuesday, January 11, in Henry's arms. He was twenty-seven. We have few details about his passing, but it was probably not peaceful. In many tetanus cases the rigidity spreads, often affecting the neck, then bends a person over backward, as depicted in a terrifying painting by Dr. Charles Bell, *Tetanus Following Gunshot Wounds* (1809). Henry is reported to have told a friend that John "was perfectly calm, even pleasant while reason lasted, and gleams of the same serenity and playfulness shone through his delirium to the last." The references to "while reason lasted" and "delirium" suggest that Henry was putting a good face on a scene that was *not* all calm and serene.

John had never been in good health. Three years older than Henry, John was of short stature, frail and thin, weighing just 117 pounds. In marked contrast with his brother Henry, John was quiet, genial, and neat. He had frequent nosebleeds, some of which, occurring when he was eighteen or so, were so

violent they made him faint. He was often sick, calling his condition "colic," but the underlying problem
was tuberculosis. He found teaching a strain, and he
and Henry had to close their little Concord school
in 1841 because of John's poor health.

After John died, Henry walked to his friend
Emerson's house, where he had stayed occasionally before John became ill. It was snowing; the
thermometer registered 32 degrees Fahrenheit.
Henry went to talk with Emerson and would talk
to no one else. Next morning he came back, collected some clothes he had left at the house, told
Lidian he didn't know when he'd be back, and left
for the Thoreau family home. With John's death,
Henry's journal stopped abruptly.

7. I Had Hoped to Be Spared This

Thoreau made no journal entries for the next five
weeks, though the wide world rolled on. On January 11, the same day John died, William James was
born in New York City, and would soon receive a
visit from Emerson, a friend of William's father.
On January 13, Dr. William Bryden, the sole sur-
vivor of a British Indian army of 4,500 men, stag-
gered into Jalalabad in India following the cata-

strophic "retreat" from Kabul, during which the entire invading army had been wiped out in the mountain passes of Afghanistan. On January 22, Charles Dickens and his wife arrived in Boston by ship from Liverpool and were met by a dozen newspaper editors who swarmed aboard for interviews. On the same day, the Thoreau family in Concord was shocked and horrified as John's younger brother Henry suddenly developed symptoms of lockjaw himself.

Henry had not cut himself, his skin was not broken, and tetanus is not contagious. Henry's illness was a two-day sympathetic reaction, an emotional response not unheard of even then. Emerson reported to his brother William on January 24 that Henry was better. But the terrible January was not over.

That same evening, Emerson's five-year-old son Waldo contracted scarlet fever, a disease for which, like tetanus, no vaccination or treatment existed at the time. By January 27, the child was delirious. When his mother, Lidian, asked Concord's Dr. Bartlett, who had made a house call, if Waldo would soon be better, he responded, "I had hoped to be spared this." A few hours later, at 8:15 in the evening, the little boy died.

The grief in the Emerson house was all-consuming. When nine-year-old Louisa May Alcott came to the door to inquire after Waldo, she was met by his thirty-eight-year-old father. Emerson was so stricken he could not bring himself to speak the name either of his boy or the girl at the door. "Child, he is dead," was all he could manage. Alcott later said this was her first experience of a great grief.

But Emerson wrote at least ten letters immediately—four that same night—pulling himself together by forcing himself to turn outward toward others. "I comprehend nothing of the fact [of Waldo's death] but its bitterness. Explanation I have none. Consolation, none that arises out of the fact itself: only diversion: only oblivion of this, and pursuit of new objects."[2]

In the Thoreau household, there was silence and a terrible inactivity. Henry was unable to get out of bed for four long weeks, and while he did return to his journal on February 19, it was a week more before he could write any letters. When he finally resumed correspondence, the letters had a preternatural calm. And the journal entries that preceded them carried a forced quality.

8. On Every Side Is
Depth Unfathomable

Thoreau's first journal entry after John's death, made on Saturday, February 19 (and it really does seem to be the first, not just the first that has survived), is a mistrustful, rather grim set of observations on a recent visit, almost certainly by Emerson. "I never yet saw two men sufficiently great to meet as two," Thoreau writes, focusing on his relationship to Emerson and bypassing the expected conventional expression of regret or sadness for each other's recent losses. "When two approach to meet they incur no petty dangers, but they run terrible risks. Between the sincere there will be no civilities," Thoreau goes on. He means there must be honesty and sincerity. Maybe civilities were extraneous for Thoreau at this low moment. Sincerity was its own reward, but it had other benefits, too. It seems highly likely that on this first trip on February 19 to see the stricken Henry, Emerson brought him a book just published by Elizabeth Peabody, Guillaume Oegger's *The True Messiah*, for this is what Thoreau was reading and taking notes on the next day, Sunday, February 20.

Oegger was a Swedenborgian who believed that because everything in nature stands for something in mind, the entire physical world then functions as a visible language, a collection of emblems we can decipher. (Swedenborg would be a huge influence on Henry James Sr., the father of William and Henry.) That Thoreau was now reading Oegger is a small signal that he was starting to get back on track. Emerson probably intended—or at least hoped—as much. And indeed, the idea that nature is a language we can learn to read would stay with Thoreau right up to the last entry he ever made in his journal about how we can see, in the gravel of the railroad beds after a storm or a rain, how each rain and wind is self-registering.[3]

The brief bit from Oegger that Thoreau entered in his journal for February 20, 1842, is positive in its understanding of a connection between nature and mind, but the entry (clearly inspired by Emerson's visit and his gift of the Oegger volume) is not typical of Thoreau's state of mind in that February week. Far from positive, Thoreau's mood was querulous, grouchy, self-critical. "It is vain to talk," he grumbles in his journal. "What do you want? To bandy words—or deliver some grains of truth which stir within you? Will you make a pleasant rumbling sound after feasting for digestion's sake? Or such music as the birds in springtime."[4]

Thoreau feels displaced just now, and unsure even of his unsureness. The next day, February 21, he writes in his journal, "I must confess there is nothing so strange to me as my own body. I love any other piece of nature, almost, better." It's that "almost" that signals trouble. And there is more trouble in his preternatural sensitivity to sound: "I was always conscious of sounds in nature which my ear could never hear . . . she always retreats as I advance." Usually so perfectly attuned to sounds, especially natural or musical, Thoreau now feels untuned, even lost: "I never saw to the end nor heard to the end but the best part was unseen— and unheard." This is not the usual "heard melodies are sweet but those unheard are sweeter," not a recurring Platonism, but, as befits someone who loved real, actual sounds, a feeling of being lost, unable to hear something all the way to the end. And not only lost, but weightless: "I feel like a feather floating in the atmosphere, on every side is depth unfathomable."

9. Only Nature Has a Right to Grieve Perpetually

A month after little Waldo's death and six weeks after brother John's demise, Henry is, in February 1842, still alienated, profoundly unsure of both his present situation and his future direction: "I have lived ill for the most part because too near myself. I have tripped myself up. . . . I cannot walk conveniently and pleasantly but when I hold myself far off in the horizon."[5]

This is not wisdom; it is not self-knowledge. It is confusion, a wild thrashing about in a bog with no bottom. But not for long. It is with a sense of relief and steadiness that we find Thoreau once again reading Chaucer on February 23 and saying, "the reader has great confidence in Chaucer." This also suggests that Thoreau had recovered his confidence in his own reading. We are further reassured to find him writing in his journal about treating or esteeming each other not for what we are, but for what we are capable of being. It feels like a return to solid ground to discover him saying, "true politeness is only hope and trust in men" and remarking on "the innate civility of nature."

By the beginning of March, the wild, distraught tone is mostly gone from Thoreau's journal (or from what he allowed to survive when he copied over earlier entries), and on March 2, there is both a long, thoughtful journal entry and a long and revealing letter to Lidian Emerson's older sister, Lucy Jackson Brown—a letter setting out, for the first time, in a direct communication to another person, what he was finally able to make of the terrible events of January.

He tells Lucy, with the unnecessary honesty of the self-involved young man, "when I realize what has transpired, and the greatness of the part I am unconsciously acting, I am thrilled, and it seems as if there were none in history to match it." This, and everything that follows in this letter, were intended for a person Thoreau felt close to and understood by. He was not writing for the editors of his Collected Correspondence, and it is easy enough to imagine—and even hope for—his scissoring away such lines before people like me got their interpretive hands on them.

The body of this letter to Lucy is as soul-baring as any he was to write, and it shows that he has now reached a strongly held, or at least convincingly expressed, acceptance of the deaths of brother John and little Waldo. He begins with the problem of grief: "What right have I to grieve, who have not ceased to wonder?" Grief is what we expect after a death. Thoreau acknowledges this:

> We feel at first as if some opportunities of kindness and sympathy were lost, but learn afterward that any *pure grief* [his italics] is ample recompense for all. That is, if we are faithful;— for a just grief is but sympathy with the soul that disposes events, and is as natural as the resin on Arabian trees. Only nature has a right to grieve perpetually, for she only is innocent.

Not only innocent but, importantly, enduring. "Soon the ice will melt," Thoreau continues addressing Lucy, "and the blackbirds sing along the river which he [John] frequented, as pleasantly as ever. The same everlasting serenity will appear in the face of God, and we will not be sorrowful if he is not."[6] Individuals die; nature lives on. This is easy to say, but if it is really meant—lived, felt—it *is* thrilling. And Thoreau sounds as though he really does mean it:

> I do not wish to see John ever again—I mean him who is dead—but that other whom only he would have wished to see, or to be, of whom he was the imperfect representative. For we are not

what we are, nor do we treat or esteem each other for such, but for what we are capable of being.

Thoreau also told Lucy in this same letter about the death of five-year-old Waldo Emerson:

As for Waldo, he died as the mist rises from the brook, which the sun will soon dart his rays through. Do not the flowers die every autumn? He had not even taken root here. I was not startled to hear that he was dead; it seemed the most natural event that could happen. His fine organization demanded it, and nature gently yielded its request. It would have been strange if he had lived.

Then Thoreau repeats the line of thought he had applied to John's death: "Neither will nature manifest any sorrow at *his* [emphasis added] death, but soon the note of the lark will be heard down in the meadow, and fresh dandelions will spring from the old stocks where he plucked them last summer."[7]

10. Death Is the Law of New Life

We can see a little further into Thoreau's inner condition at this moment by reading a journal entry he made the same day he wrote the words above to Lucy Brown: "The greatest impression of character is made by that person who consents to have no character. He who sympathizes with and runs through the whole circle of attributes can not afford to be an individual." This is a great statement of the kind of negative capability Keats is famous for describing. It suggests that the problem with Thoreau's reaction to these personal losses is not too little feeling but too much. Physically, literally, the deaths of John and Waldo knocked him flat. But emotionally they connected him more solidly than ever with nature, with the rivers, the fields, and the forest.

Six days after the letter and the journal entry we have just reviewed, Thoreau—again in the journal—arrived at a kind of summing up. The entry reads:

> I live in the perpetual verdure of the globe. I die in the annual decay of nature. We can understand the phenomenon of death in the animal better if we first consider it in the order next below us [shades of Swedenborg!] the vegetable. The death of the flea and the Elephant are but phenomena of the life of nature.[8]

The clarity, the tone, the simplicity, and the deftly itemized list all suggest that this was the

real turning point for Thoreau, the turn from seeing the world made up of irreplaceable individuals to seeing it as a huge whole of which everything and everyone is just a tiny piece. At this
point, then, and not before, Thoreau was finally
able to address Emerson himself. Emerson was
away from Concord, fulfilling obligations to lecture in New York City and looking in on the new-
born William James, so Thoreau wrote him a letter on March 11, three days after the journal entry
"I live. . . . I die."

The letter is entirely devoted to the death of
Waldo, though Thoreau cannot name him any
more than Emerson could when facing little Louisa Alcott. A major earlier turning point in Thoreau's life had been his reading of Emerson's *Nature*, and Thoreau now addresses Emerson on just
that subject:

Nature is not ruffled by the rudest blast. The
hurricane only snaps a few twigs in some nook
of the forest. The snow attains its average depth
each winter, and the chic-a-dee lisps the same
notes. The old laws prevail in spite of pesti-
lence and famine. No genius or virtue so rare
and revolutionary appears in town or village,

that the pine ceases to exude resin in the wood, or beast or bird lays aside its habits.[9]

Having laid the groundwork, Thoreau pushes on:

How plain that death is only the phenomenon of the individual or class. Nature does not recognize it. She finds her own again under new forms without loss. Yet death is beautiful when seen to be a law, and not an accident—It is as common as life. . . . Every blade in the field— every leaf in the forest—lays down its life in its season as beautifully as it was taken up.

When we look over the fields we are not saddened because these particular flowers or grasses will wither—for their death is the law of new life. . . . One might as well go into mourning for every sere leaf—but the more innocent and wiser soul will snuff a fragrance in the gales of autumn and congratulate nature on her health.[10]

The next paragraph, the last except for six valedictory lines from a Scottish poet, acknowledges the gap between imagining how things should be and how they really are: "After I have imagined thus much will not the Gods feel under obligation to make me realize something as good?"

Over the next couple of days, Thoreau worked to hold this focus, and to deepen, sharpen, and clarify what he now saw. The next day, March 12, we find him writing in his journal, "To die is not to *begin* to die—and *continue*—it is not a state of continuance but of transientness. . . . There is no continuance of death—it is a transient phenomenon— Nature presents nothing in a state of death."[11] Seventeen years later Thoreau would sharpen this insight, writing in his journal for February 3, 1859:

> I perceive that we partially die ourselves through sympathy at the death of each of our friends or near relatives. Each such experience is an assault on our vital force. It becomes a source of wonder that they who have lost many friends still live. After long watching around the sickbed of a friend, we, too, partially give up the ghost with him, and are the less to be identified with this state of things.

But on Sunday, March 13, 1842, Thoreau was reaching a vision of things that would be restated

in the twentieth century by Alfred North Whitehead. Thoreau says:

> There seem to be two sides to this world pre-
> sented us at different times—as we see things
> in growth or dissolution—in life or death—
> For seen with the eye of a poet—as God sees
> them, all are alive and beautiful, but seen with
> the historical eye, or the eye of the memory, they
> are dead and offensive. If we see nature as paus-
> ing, immediately all mortifies and decays—but
> seen as progressing she is beautiful.[12]

Whitehead put it this way in *The Function of
Reason* (1929):

> History discloses two main tendencies in the
> course of events. One tendency is exemplified
> in the slow decay of nature. With stealthy inevi-
> tableness, there is degradation of energy. The
> sources of activity sink downward and down-
> ward. Their very matter wastes. The other ten-
> dency is exemplified by the yearly renewal of
> nature in the spring. . . . Reason is the self-
> discipline of the originative element in history.

Thoreau's own fullest, best-expressed explanation of how these two forces act on each other, on

how death becomes life, is in the "Spring" chapter of *Walden*. As the book is gathering force toward a conclusion, the prose is different from the unconvincing flights of Thoreau's letter to Emerson on the death of little Waldo. Now Thoreau's prose is at ease with its subject, ending, as so often in the mature Thoreau's writing, with a sardonic chuckle or two:

> There was a dead horse in the hollow by the path to my house, which compelled me sometimes to go out of my way, especially in the night when the air was heavy, but the assurance it gave me of the strong appetite and inviolable health of Nature was my compensation for this. I love to see that nature is so rife with life that myriads can afford to be sacrificed and suffered to prey on one another; that tender organizations can be so serenely squashed out of existence like pulp,—tadpoles which herons gobble up, and tortoises and toads run over in the road; and that sometimes it has rained flesh and blood! With the liability to accident, we must see how little account is to be made of it. The impression on a wise man is that of universal innocence. Poison is not poisonous after all,

nor are any wounds fatal [not even John's!].
Compassion is a very untenable ground. It
must be expeditious. Its pleadings will not bear
to be stereotyped.

11. My Friend Is My Real Brother

Thoreau's affirmation of 1842 is either real (really
felt) or put on (bluster). Its clarity argues for its
being real for Thoreau, as does his casting around
for the right way to put it. "What," he writes in his
journal on March 12, "if you or I be dead—God is
alive still." And the next day, in a letter to another
old friend, Thoreau says, "The soul which does
shape the world is within and central."

Thoreau, in 1842, sees the dreadful events of
the past two and a half months not as an ending,
but as a beginning. Though he feels good for little
but counting "how many eggs the hens lay" and
bringing the news, he also smiles and admits, "I
expect my life will begin."[13] To his friend Isaiah
Williams he is just as hopeful: "My destiny is now
arrived—is now arriving. I believe that what I call
my circumstances will be a very true history of
myself."[14]

This world view, or, more accurately, this view of the two great opposed forces in nature, which Thoreau reaches in mid-March 1842, is nothing less than his mature philosophical vision. The two forces are entropy, as it plays out in "Fall" and "Winter," and the originative element—the life force—behind "Spring." The relation between these two is best put by Emerson, who says in "The Poet" (a subject on which he was lecturing and working around this time, as it happens), "Genius is the activity that repairs the decay of things." Resilience is less splashy than genius, but has—or can have—the same result.

Thoreau had come to this way of seeing the world more or less on his own during the two months since John's death. And when he was at last able to jot it down in his journal as a solid, arrived-at, personal understanding of nature, the solidity of the conclusion seems to have taken some of the self-generated pressure off Thoreau, allowing him to return to something like ordinary life. On March 15, 1842, the day after the entropy-creativity entry in his journal, Thoreau managed to get out and off "to the woods."[15] On the March 17, he was back to helping his father make pencils.

After work that day, he "walked to see an old schoolmate."[16] On the next day, the eighteenth, Emerson returned to Concord from his lecture tour in New York City. On March 19, Thoreau was again walking in the fields. At some point around this time, probably on the same day, he and Emerson met, for on March 20 there is a long entry in Thoreau's journal on friendship and a friend who is not named, but who can only be Emerson:

> My friend is cold and reserved because his love for me is waxing and not waning. These are the early processes—the particles are just beginning to shoot in crystals. If the mountains came to me I should no longer go to the mountains—So soon as that consummation takes place which I wish—it will be past—Shall I not have a friend in reserve? Heaven is to come. I hope this is not it.

Friendship itself is now a process of nature, and that last sentence shows that Thoreau's sense of humor has returned. But he is far from finished with the topic. Later in the same journal entry we find him insisting, "We do not wish friends to feed and clothe our bodies—neighbors are kind enough for that—but to do the like offices to our-selves." He has been writing about the importance of telling a friend just where you found a fact that makes a difference. "We wish to spread and pub-lish ourselves—as the sun spreads its rays," he continues, "and we toss the new thought to the friend and thus it is dispersed. Friends are those twain who feel their interests to be one—Each knows that the other might as well have said what he said. All beauty—all music—all delight springs from apparent dualism—but real unity."

Rereading this, Thoreau added, in pencil, "My friend is my real brother." The paragraph then ends, "I see his nature groping yonder so like mine— Does there go one whom I know then I go there."[17]

12. Emerson Commissions a Book Review

Emerson must have been immensely buoyed by the kinds of things Thoreau was now able to put in words—the powerful, positive vision of au-tumnal decay versus the springing of the year, for example. Thoreau could see the effect he had on Emerson. "The friend does not take my word for any think [*sic*]—but he takes me—He trusts me as I trust myself," Thoreau wrote: "We only need to be as true to others as we are to ourselves that there may be ground enough for Friendship."[18]

Something has now healed in Thoreau, enabling him to say, astonishingly, "my friend is my real brother." Something must have healed at this point in Emerson as well. Approaching age thirty-nine, successful as a writer and lecturer, with two small children and a wife at home, and two books, *Nature* and *Essays, First Series* (including "History" "Self-Reliance," and "Compensation") behind him, he was just now taking over as editor of the *Dial*. Margaret Fuller, the *Dial*'s first editor, had written Emerson in mid-March 1842, to say she just couldn't continue. Emerson, with wry and characteristic humor, had agreed to take over. "Let there be rotation in martyrdom," he said.

A couple of weeks after the meeting that produced Thoreau's outpouring on friendship, Emerson handed Thoreau a pile of books and an assignment to write a review of them for the *Dial*. Among the publications that had started coming Emerson's way, now that he was the editor of a magazine, were Colman's *Fourth Report on the Agricul-*

ture of Massachusetts, and a series of "Reports—on the Fishes, Reptiles and Birds, the Herbaceous Plants and Quadrupeds, the Insects injurious to Vegetation and the Invertebrate Animals of Massachusetts." The reports had been authorized by the state legislature and published by the Commissioners on the Zoological and Botanical Surveys of Massachusetts.

Emerson held on to Colman's Agriculture report, which he read and commented on in his journal, but he forwarded the others to Thoreau in early April.[19]

Emerson would not have expected Thoreau to write a conventional book review of such work-a-day documents, but he was confident that the material would give the younger man a chance to show off his "woodcraft, boatcraft, and fishcraft." He must have thought Thoreau would be as pleased with the volumes as he himself was. "Last night I read many pages in Chester Dewey's Report of Herbaceous plants in Massachusetts," Emerson wrote: "With what delight we always come to these images! The mere names of reeds and grasses, of the milk weeds, of the mint tribe and the gentians, of mallows and trefoils, are a lively pleasure."[20]

The Natural History of Massachusetts

What Thoreau did with these reports, and did pretty quickly, was to write a review essay called "Natural History of Massachusetts," published in the *Dial* in July 1842. It is Thoreau's first major piece of writing, the moment when, as Laura Walls puts it in her splendid biography, "Henry D. Thoreau finally entered the room."

Like a typical *New York Review of Books* piece today, "Natural History of Massachusetts" is an independent, personal essay on the *subjects* of the books under consideration. The books themselves are mentioned only at the end of the "review," and disparagingly at that. "These volumes," Thoreau says, "deal much in measurements and minute descriptions not interesting to the general reader." What we have instead of a review is a self-standing piece on the fundamental and all-important health of the natural world.

For his opening sentence, indeed the opening paragraph, Thoreau goes back to the passage he had written in his journal on Friday, December 31, 1841, *just one day* before John cut himself while shaving. It is as though Thoreau was reaching back to pick up a dropped link, to bridge over the

troubles of January–March 1842. The passage
Thoreau chooses to start the essay begins:

> Books of natural history make the most cheer-
> ful winter reading. I read in Audubon with a
> thrill of delight when the snow covers the ground
> of the magnolia and the Florida keys and their
> warm sea-breezes—of the fence rail and the
> cotton tree and the migrations of the rice-bird—
> or of the breaking up of winter in Labrador. I
> seem to hear the melting of the snow on the
> forks of the Missouri as I read. I imbibe some
> portion of health from these reminiscences of
> luxuriant nature. There is a singular health for
> me in those words Labrador and East Main—
> which no desponding creed recognizes.

The first three paragraphs of the "Natural History
of Massachusetts"—including all the best phrases
and sentences—come from the one long journal
entry—only partially quoted here—of December 31, 1841.

One of the things we learn from this is that the
emphasis on health in "Natural History of Massachusetts" is not something Thoreau included
because of John's and Waldo's illnesses and
death—though that emphasis may be *needed* now

more than ever. No, the belief in health, in the persistence of health, was there in Thoreau all along, needing not to be discovered but recovered.

If the prose of "Natural History of Massachusetts" is not yet so good as it will be in *Walden*, there are sentences in the essay as good as any Thoreau will ever write. Some are famous, some not. The line "Surely joy is the condition of life," which can be found on countless refrigerator magnets, occurs in the third paragraph. To understand the deep trouble out of which, and against which, this piece was written, ask yourself why this sentence needs the word *surely*. "What an admirable training is science for the more active warfare of life" is a sentence that deserves to be better known, as does "How much more than federal are these states."

Structure will always be a problem for Thoreau. In this essay, he takes a few false steps. In one he gives the reader a long, Anacreontic poem beginning

> Behold how spring appearing
> The Graces send forth roses.

Thoreau leaves these (and many more) saccharine verses in the main body of the essay and relegates to a mere footnote his sharp-eyed and much more interesting observation of a robin's nest set "upon the end of a board in the loft of a sawmill, but a few feet from the saw, which [nest] vibrated several inches with the motion of the machinery."

But such lapses are rare. Mostly Thoreau catches and holds our attention, often with his uncanny sensitivity to sounds: "The nuthatch and chicadee flitting in company through the dells of the wood, the one harshly scolding at the intruder, the other with a faint lisping note enticing him on, the jay screaming in the orchard, the crow cawing in unison with the storm."[21]

Perhaps the single most important thing in this essay is the first clear appearance in Thoreau's writing of a point of view that goes beyond the anthropocentric to an ecocentric or nature-centered vision. Here is the passage:

The fish-hawk, too, is occasionally seen at this season [Spring] sailing majestically over the water, and he who has once observed it will not soon forget the majesty of its flight. It sails the air like a ship of the line, worthy to struggle with the elements, falling back from time to time like a ship on its beam ends, and holding its talons up, as if ready for the arrows, in the attitude of the national bird. It is a great presence, as of the master of river and forest. Its eye would not quail before the owner of the soil, but make him feel like an intruder on its domains.[22]

This way of seeing is one kind of negative capability, negative in the sense of negating the self. It is an imaginative projection or empathic identification with the "other"—in this case, other beings in nature. This way of seeing is one of the best things Thoreau has for us, and it will be a steady presence in his writing from now on, from the "Natural History of Massachusetts" right up through *Walden*, more than a dozen years ahead, where we will again come upon Henry Thoreau out watching another hawk, in the next-to-last chapter, "Spring." The passage is long but well worth it:

On the 29th of April, as I was fishing from the bank of the river near the Nine-Acre-Corner bridge, standing on the quaking grass and willow roots, where the muskrats lurk, I heard a singular rattling sound, somewhat like that of the sticks which boys play with their fingers, when, looking up, I observed a very slight and graceful hawk, like a night-hawk, alternately soaring like a ripple and tumbling a rod or two over and over, showing the underside of its wings, which gleamed like a satin ribbon in the sun, or like the pearly inside of a shell. . . . It was the most ethereal flight I had ever witnessed. It did not simply flutter like a butterfly, nor soar like the larger hawks, but it sported with proud reliance in the fields of air; mounting again and again with its strange chuckle, it repeated its free and beautiful fall, turning over and over like a kite, and then recovering from its lofty tumbling, as if it had never set its foot on *terra firma*. It appeared to have no companion in the universe,—sporting there alone,—and to need none but the morning and the ether with which it played. It was not lonely but made all the earth lonely beneath it.

What makes this scene work is the long, detailed, and completely believable description of the hawk from the point of view of the man on the riverbank, followed by the single breathtaking sentence that leaps up to see the earth from the hawk's point of view. For a moment, man is not the lord of creation; the hawk is.

13. Our Own Limits Transgressed

Thoreau's great work, his major period, and some
of the best material for his masterpiece, *Walden*,
begins with the "Natural History of Massachusetts" (July 1842), which in turn grew out of the
sudden, awful, and unexpected deaths of January 1842. During that month and the two that followed, Thoreau arrived at and expressed three
crucial ingredients of his mature vision of the
world. All three of these realizations cut against
the sentimentalism of his day—and ours—and
they help account for the stiffness some readers
still find in Thoreau's writing. First, he realized
that our intellectual connections and our friend-
ships actually matter more than family. Thoreau's
disindividualizing a brother's death coincided
with recognizing a bond stronger than brother-
hood, namely friendship. We do not choose our
kin; we can and do choose our friends. What looks
at first like Thoreau's coldest shoulder—accepting
the deaths of John and Waldo—is somehow an-
swered or completed by his realization and acceptance that "my friend is my real brother."

Second, during this time he also saw that despite
the death and disease and decay of the individual,

the natural world as a whole, and at its micro-
scopic level, is fundamentally healthy. People die
and life goes on. Death is a necessary part of life.

The third realization, now first fully articulated,
is that we need an anti-anthropomorphic, nature-
centered vision of how things are. Thoreau's
growing friendship with Emerson was the direct
cause of the first of these three realizations, and it
was the likely catalyst for the other two. The result
is nothing less than the sudden emergence of the
greatest American voice yet for the natural world,
a world including—but not centered on—us.

The short period from Thoreau's collapse to his
first major piece of writing also says a lot about
Thoreau's own resilience. Where Emerson's recovery took more than a year and involved several
different breaks with his past, Thoreau's path to
recovery involved a *re*-validation, through brutal
experiences, of ideas and ties he already had before John's death, and to which he returned after
severe but short-term testing.

The last paragraph of "Natural History of Massachusetts" points the way to *Walden*: "The true
man of science will know nature better by his
finer organization; he will smell, taste, see, hear,
feel, better than other men. His will be a deeper

and finer experience. We do not learn by inference and deduction, and the application of mathematics to philosophy, but by direct intercourse and sympathy."[23] And toward the end of *Walden* he addresses the same subject, showing us where "direct intercourse and sympathy" have taken him:

> We can never have enough of Nature. We must be refreshed by the sight of inexhaustible vigor, vast and Titanic features, the sea-coast with its wrecks, the wilderness with its living and its decaying trees, the thunder cloud, and the rain which lasts three weeks and produces freshets. We need to witness our own limits transgressed, and some life pasturing freely where we never wander.[24]

The arc of Emerson's resilient recovery from his collapse after Ellen's death covers a little more than two and a half years, from February 1831 to November 1833, and it provoked major life changes. Emerson went from a focus on theology to a focus on science, from life as a minister to life as a public lecturer, from Boston to Concord. The Emerson who gave the "Uses of Natural History" talk in November 1833 was a very different man from the pastor who had delivered "The Lord's Supper" in September 1832.

The arc of Thoreau's recovery, from John's death in January 1842 to the publication of "The Natural History of Massachusetts" in the *Dial* for July 1842, spans just six months and resulted in neither a change of subject nor profession. Instead, the process involved a deepening, a rethinking and revalidation of an approach to nature that Thoreau had already held in a general way before John's death. But what had been a more or less conventional romantic approach to nature quickly became, after John's death, a profoundly felt emotional acceptance—not just an intellectual assent—of death as an inescapable part of living, and an acceptance that at some level, there is no death. The very process of decay is a life process. The consequences of this view—of believing, not just mouthing—is to understand and accept a disindividualized view of life. The individual may die, but the materials that make up the individual do not. They are subsumed into new forms and so live on. This view, if one can grasp and hold it, means that in a general or communal sense, there is no death. This conviction, once firmly accepted, is, paradoxically, a powerful force for individual resilience. The wide-awake individual now knows that his or her resilience is not idiosyncratic but something held in common with all other people and all other forms of life, and derives its power from the very fact that it *is* common.

Part III

William James

If this life be not a real fight, in which something is gained for the universe by success, it is no better than a game of private theatricals from which one may withdraw at will. But it *feels* like a real fight, as if there were something really wild in the universe, which we, with all our idealities and faithfulnesses, are needed to redeem, and first of all to redeem our own hearts from atheisms and fears. For such a half-wild half-saved universe our nature is adapted.

—WILLIAM JAMES, FROM *THE WILL TO BELIEVE*

14. The Death of Minny Temple

In July 1868, when William James was twenty-six, he was full of despair, writing in his diary, "Tu veux mourir, hien? Parce que chez toi il y a tant des choses qui ne mènent a rien, et qui ne sont que dégoutantes" (So you want to die, is that it? Because with you there are so many things that lead to nothing and which are nothing but disgusting).[1] A year and a half later he was still despairing when, in January 1870, he received a letter from his twenty-four-year-old cousin, Minny Temple. Most of the letter is missing, but the fragment that remains says a lot in a few words:

> [beginning of letter missing] filment, this Christianity would seem to be the only comfort—& the more that I live the more I feel there *must be* some comfort somewhere for the mass of people, suffering and sad, outside of that which Stoicism gives—A thousand times when I see a poor person in trouble, it almost breaks my heart that I can't say something to them to comfort them. It is on the tip of my tongue to say it, and I

can't, for I have always felt the unutterable
sadness & mystery that envelopes us
all—I shall take some of your Chloral
tonight, if I don't sleep. Don't let my
letter of yesterday make you feel that we
are not very near to each other—friends
at heart. Altho' practically being much
with you or even writing to you would
not be good for me—Too much strain
on one key will make it snap—& there
is an *attitude* of mind, (not a strength of
Intellect by any means) in which we are
much alike—Goodbye—

> Your aff. Cousin/
> Mary Temple[2]

Two months later, on March 8, 1870, Minny
Temple died of tuberculosis. She was twenty-
four. William James noted her death in his journal
as he noted no other, with a simple line drawing
of a headstone marked with the initials M. T. Two
weeks after Minny's death, William wrote a sort
of goodbye to her in his journal:

By that big part of me that's in the tomb with you,
may I realize and believe in the immediacy of

death. Minny, your death makes me feel the nothingness of all our egotistical fury. The inevitable release is sure; wherefore take our turn kindly, whatever it contains. Ascend to some sort of partnership with fate, and since tragedy is at the heart of us, go to meet it, work it to our ends, instead of dodging it all our days, and being run down by it at last. Use your death (or your life, it's all one meaning) *tat tvam asi.*[3]

That last phrase is Sanskrit, from one of the oldest Upanishads, the Chandogya. *Tat* means *ultimate reality*, and *tvam* is *the individual self.* The phrase asserts that the two are similar, maybe the same. You are not just in the world; you and the world are the same thing. William James was twenty-eight when he wrote this.

15. Minny and Henry

Before we can ask how James recovered from this knockdown loss, we need to ask who Minny Temple was, and how she came to have the effect on William (and on William's brother Henry as well) that she did. Minny Temple was simply and without question the most interesting, most intense, most intelligent young woman that William and Henry knew. Many years later, in 1914, in the second volume of Henry's memoirs, *Notes of a Son and Brother*, the entire last chapter, fifty-seven printed pages, is an account of Minny as the consummate heroine of his and William's youth:

> Everything that took place around her took place as if primarily in relation to her and in her interest: that is in the interest of drawing her out and displaying her the more. This too without her in the least caring . . . whether such an effect took place or not.[4]

She was a cousin, the daughter of Henry James Sr.'s sister Catherine. Her rule of life was believing in "the remote possibility of the best things being better than a clear certainty of the second best."[5] "She had," Henry recalled, "beyond any equally young creature I have known a sense for verity of character and play of life in others, for their acting out of their force or weakness, whatever either might be, at no matter what cost to herself: and it was this instinct that made her care so for life in general, just as it was her being thereby so engaged in that tangle that made her, as I have expressed it, ever the heroine of the scene."[6] Looking back forty-four years, from a new century, Henry's image of Minny and her incomparable gifts remained vivid: "The charming, the irresistible fact was that one had never seen a creature with such lightness of forms, a lightness all her own, so inconsequently grave at the core, or an asker of endless questions with such apparent lapses of care."

In his 1914 memoir, Henry gives an account of his last meeting with Minny:

Singularly present has remained to "Harry," as may be imagined, the rapid visit he paid her at Pelham that February [1869]; he was spending a couple of days in New York, on a quick decision, before taking ship for England. I ["he" and "I" are the same person in this helplessly personal account] was then to make in Europe no such stay as she had forecast—I was away but for fifteen months; though I can well believe my appetite must have struck her as open to the boundless, and can easily be touched again by her generous thought of this as the right compensatory thing for me. That indeed is what I mainly recall of the hour I spent with her—so unforgettable nonetheless in its general value; our so beautifully agreeing that quite the same course would be the right thing for her and that it was wholly detestable that I should be voyaging off without her. But the precious question and the bright aspect of her own still waiting chance made our talk for the time all gaiety; it was strangely enough, a laughing hour altogether, colored with the vision of the next winter in Rome, where we should romantically meet; the appearance then being of particular protective friends with Roman designs, under whose wing she might happily travel. She had at that moment been for many weeks as ill as will here have been shown: but such is the priceless good faith of youth that we perfectly kept at bay together the significance of this.

Henry's description has photographic detail. Thinking back on how ill Minny really was, he goes on:

I recall no mortal note—nothing but the bright extravagance of her envy; and see her again, in the old-time Pelham parlours, ever so erectly slight, and so more than needfully, so transparently, fair (I fatuously took this for "becoming"),

glide as swiftly, toss her head as characteristi-
cally, laugh to as free a disclosure of the hand-
some largish teeth that made her mouth almost
the main fact of her face, as if no corner of the
veil of the future had been lifted.[7]

When Minny died, Henry James was twenty-six
and living abroad. He received the sad news in a
letter from his mother. He wrote her, and immediately wrote William as well. Henry's initial reaction
to Minny's death is remarkably similar to Thoreau's
response to the death of little Waldo: "A few short
hours have amply sufficed to more than reconcile
me to the event & to make it seem the most
natural—the happiest, fact in her whole career." To
be sure, he balanced this quickly, saying, "So it
seems, at least, on reflection; to the eye of feeling
there is something immensely moving in the sudden
and complete extinction of a vitality so exquisite &
so apparently infinite as Minny's." Then he reverts
to his first response: "But what most occupies me,
as it will have done all of you at home, is the thought
of how her whole life seemed to tend & hasten,
visibly, audibly, sensibly, to that consummation."[8]

At age twenty-six, Henry already had a strong
sense of just how unusual Minny was. He goes on,

in this same letter to William: "what strikes me above all is how great and rare a benefit her life has been to those with whom she was associated. I feel as if a very fair portion of my sense of the reach and quality and capacity of human nature rested upon my experience of her character."[9]

All the young men who knew Minny were thought to be "in love" with her, though that seems too flat a phrase and too simple a description of the extraordinary interest she aroused in Henry and William James, in Oliver Wendell Holmes Jr., and in John Gray (co-founder of the Boston law firm Ropes and Gray). As Henry James noted in his long letter to William about Minny's death, "Every one was supposed I believe to be more or less in love with her: others may answer for themselves: I never was, & yet I had the great satisfaction that I enjoyed *pleasing* her almost as much as if I had been."[10]

In fact, Henry registered Minny's death as a major loss: "I have been hearing all my life of the sense of loss wh[ich] death leaves behind it— now for the first time I have a chance to learn what it amounts to."[11] He was afraid, as Emerson had been afraid, of losing the sense of loss, of being so shallow as to be able to forget. Henry continues, in the letter to William, "you will have felt for yourself I suppose how little is the utmost one can *do*, in a positive sense, as regards her memory. Her presence was so much, so intent— so strenuous—so full of human exaction; her absence is so modest, so content with so little. A little decent passionless grief—a little rummage in our little store of wisdom—a sigh of relief— and we begin to live for ourselves again."[12]

We shall soon see how William dealt with Minny's death. But in some sense, Henry never did get over it. Minny shows up in Henry's fiction. Parts of her are in Isabel Archer in *Portrait of a Lady* and Daisy Miller in *Daisy Miller*. Milly Theale in *The Wings of the Dove* has Minny's initials.[13] And in a passage in *The Ambassadors* (1903), the main character, Strether, says to Little Bilham:

> Live all you can; it's a mistake not to. It doesn't so much matter what you do in particular so long as you have your life. If you haven't had that what have you had? . . . I haven't done so enough before—and now I'm too old; too old at any rate for what I see . . . What one loses one loses; make no mistake about that. . . . Still, we have the illusion of freedom; therefore don't be, like me,

without the memory of that illusion. I was either,
at the right time, too stupid or too intelligent to
have it; I don't quite know which. Of course at
present I'm a case of reaction against my
mistake . . . Do what you like so long as you don't
make my mistake. For it was a mistake. Live![14]

Minny's death was not a new beginning for
Henry, nor did it open a path to a new beginning. It
was a loss, plain and simple. The extraordinary last
chapter of *Notes of a Son and Brother* relives that
loss, and makes no move to put it aside or behind.
It is a frank, enduring—an endured—loss:

One may have wondered . . . what life would
have had for her and how her exquisite faculty
of challenge could have "worked in" with what
she was likely to have encountered or been
confined to. None the less did she in fact cling
to consciousness; death, at the last was dreadful to her; she would have given anything
to live—and the image of this, which was long
to remain with me, appeared so of the essence
of tragedy that I was in the far-off aftertime to
seek to lay the ghost by wrapping it, a particular occasion aiding, in the beauty and dignity
of art.[15]

Minny represented *living* for Henry in a way no-
body else quite did. In the last sentences of the
chapter, James writes, "Much as this cherished
companion's presence among us had represented
for William and myself—and it is on *his* behalf I
especially speak [William himself had been dead
for four years when Henry wrote this], her death
made a mark that must stand here for a too waiting conclusion. We felt it together as the end of
our youth."[16]

16. Minny and William

When Minny was fifteen, nearly sixteen, she cut her
hair, leaving her looking a bit boyish. This was at
a time when American women in general never
cut their hair. I have a photograph of a great-
grandmother with her back to the camera and only
a partial profile of her face looking back over her
shoulder. Her hair—which is the whole point of the
photo—flows down her back to just below her
knees. When Minny chopped hers off, young Willie
James, still a teenager, made much of it in a letter to
Minny's sister, Katherine Temple. William writes
with exaggerated horror and mock outrage at
Minny's "fearful catastrophe": "Was she all alone

when she did it? Could no one wrest the shears from her Vandal hand? I declare I fear to return home—but of course Dr Prince has her by this time."[17]

The nineteen-year-old who wrote this (and much more like it) had just decided not to study to be a painter and had gone instead to the Lawrence Scientific School in Cambridge. Three years later, at twenty-two, he entered medical school, which he interrupted the next year, 1865, to become a scientific assistant to Professor Louis Agassiz on a major expedition up the Amazon. Agassiz was seeking to refute Darwin by showing that each species was created in the exact location where it was still to be found (if the area hadn't been interfered with).

Upon his return from the Amazon, William moved with the James family to Cambridge, Massachusetts. After another long break from Harvard Medical School in 1867–1868, William received his final degree. In June 1869 he became, at age twenty-seven, William James, MD. In November of that year, Minny Temple, who still lived in Newport, Rhode Island, paid two visits to the Jameses in Cambridge. During these visits, William became much closer to and sympathetic with Minny than he ever had. In early December, William wrote his brother Henry about her. If there was no undertone of affection—or very little—in the letter the teenage William wrote to Kitty, quoted above, the letter William now wrote to Henry reads quite differently:

> M. Temple was here for a week a fortnight since. She was delightful in all respects, and, although very thin, very cheerful. I am conscious of having done her a good deal of injustice for some years past in nourishing a sort of unsympathetic hostility to her. . . . She is more devoid of "meanness," of anything petty in her character than anyone I know, perhaps either male or female.[18]

Minny was both bright and thoughtful. She could talk and write on complex subjects with ease and graceful clarity. About a week after William's letter to Henry, Minny wrote to another close friend, John Gray, "it seems to me, after all, that what comfort we get in religion, and what light we have upon it, come to us through feeling, that is through trusting our feelings, our instinct, as the voice of God."[19]

What was growing between Minny and William is difficult—maybe impossible—to know at this distance and on the surviving evidence. Courtship was probably not part of their relationship. What is clear is that somehow they were very close. They treat each other as intellectual equals, they hold nothing back, and they have a shared interest in religious experience. Minny had high standards and ideals, and relationship was very much on both their minds. In the same letter to Gray about the remote possibility of the best being preferable to a clear certainty of the second best, Minny also said, "I am aware that if all other women felt the eternal significance of marriage to the extent that I do, that hardly any of them would get married at all."[20] And just a month after Minny's visits to the Jameses in November 1869, William wrote in his diary for December 21, 1869:

I may not study, make or enjoy, but I can will. I can find some real life in the mere respect for other forms of life as they pass, even if I can never embrace them as a whole or incorporate them with myself. Nature and Life have unfitted me for any affectionate relations with other individuals—it is well to know the limits of one's individual faculties, in order not to accept intellectual[ly] the verdict of one's personal feeling and experience as the measure of objective fact—but to brood over them is morbid.[21]

Three weeks after this, on January 15, 1870, comes the stoicism letter from Minny to William: "the more I live the more I feel there *must* be some comfort somewhere for the mass of people, suffering and sad, outside of that which stoicism gives." Then, almost a month later, on February 10, Minny wrote William a full account of her religious struggle. The letter is strangely moving, starting as it does with an ominous (in retrospect) health report.

> Dearest Willy—
>
> I can't write you much of a letter, for I have been awake all night and feel very seedy—but there are one or two things I want to say to you. First, thank you most heartily for your letter [now lost] which was so much to the point—and so kind and sympathetic. Then you ask why the feeling toward and subsequently the reaction against Christianity—which I will try to explain presently.

Minny then launches into quite a lengthy explanation of her wrestling with classic American

Channing-style Unitarianism. The letter is long, but needs to be read through if we are to grasp what was really most on Minny's mind at this crucial point:

> In the meantime, I want to say that your second kind of Christianity that you speak of, is about what I have always believed, and have in it, up to this time been quite happy—but there was after all no idea of any "Atonement" about it. It was simply a belief that God had sent Christ into the world to show us how beautiful a life of unselfishness & holiness was—and a thankfulness toward Christ and love for him, because he had been true to the end—& had lived his life out, pure of any selfish motive so that mankind could ever after see the beauty of it, & be incited to do the same—that the light of his perfect life might shine before us—so that we should glorify God—& the happiness came from a feeling that if Christ could so love mankind, God must all the more & that all was right & that all it behooved us to do was not to let Christ's Sacrifice

be made in vain, by our neglecting to do
as he told us to. So that the main principle
of that belief was aspiring after perfection,
absolute perfection, as shown in Christ's
life—anything short of this Ideal would
be a practical denial of Christ—I say this
belief was a happy one for a great many
years, because I felt that I really *did want*
to follow it out & meant to some day,
more thoroughly—and in the meantime
when I saw that for the most part my life
[four pages missing].

Of course it isn't necessary to say that
I found I didn't want to do the first—in
short, I saw that I couldn't practically
live a holy Life—that even if I succeeded
in doing a given act, it was done with
weariness and grudgingly—& the *rest*
that Christ had promised his disciples
was certainly not in that ceaseless striving
after an impossible Ideal. Do you call
that feeling "separated from God" which
you ask if I felt? I don't—I call it feeling
that I must have mistaken the mission of
Christ, or else that Christianity was not
the whole of life—or else finally, the third

alternative that I was, indeed, hopelessly trifling. Then came the sleepless night that I told you of, when casting about in my mind for something or other to lay hold of I thought of what uncle Henry said that Christ didn't come that we might be unselfish & pure like him, but to show us once for all that we were selfish and impure—then followed the thought that I wrote to you about. What if there should be truth in the old Orthodox Atonement after all—a mysterious intervention of God to save us & make us happy by the *vicarious* suffering of Christ, once for all, a thing accomplished, which freed us forever from any debt except one of gratitude—something which we couldn't in the least understand, but must accept blindly as God's way of saving us—& which forever did away with any hope on our part of ever uniting ourselves with God by our own effort, but which gave us every blessing simply by our accepting Christ's mediation with humility—As I tell you, I was tired out mentally and physically then, & I saw in this idea a delusive *Rest* which was grateful to me, but which subsequently was distasteful & seemed ignominious to me. So, dear Willy, that doesn't at all satisfy me—I am after all a good deal of a pagan—certain noble acts of bygone heathen stoics & philosophers call out a quick and sympathetic response in my heart. If I had lived before Christ, Music would have come like a divine voice to tell me to be true to my whole nature— to stick to my keynote & have faith that my life would so, in some way or other, if faithfully lived, swell the entire harmony— This is a grander music than the music of the spheres. Of course the question will always remain, what is one's true life—& we must each try & solve it for ourselves. I confess that I am [end of letter missing].[22]

17. From Panic and Despair to the Acceptance of Free Will

A little less than a month later, it was over. Minny died on March 8: William learned about it the next day. On March 22, William made the entry in his journal about "the big part of me that's in the tomb with you."

Then, in April, William had an "acute neuras-
thenic attack, with phobia," as he called it. William was at this time a troubled young man, and
Minny's death added to the pressure he was putting on himself. The result, this time, was a sudden vision, a "revelation," a "horrible fear of my
own existence." So vivid was the experience that
William later included it in his *Varieties of Religious Experience*, in the section called "The Sick
Soul," though he lightly masked the source by di-
vulging it only in an endnote:

Whilst in this state of philosophic pessimism
and general depression of spirits about my
prospects, I went one evening into a dressing
room in the twilight to procure some article
that was there; when suddenly there fell upon
me without any warning, just as if it came out
of the darkness, a horrible fear of my own existence. Simultaneously there arose in my mind
the image of an epileptic patient whom I had
seen in the asylum, a black-haired youth with
greenish skin, entirely idiotic, who used to sit
all day on one of the benches, or rather shelves
against the wall, with his knees drawn up
against his chin, and the coarse grey under-
shirt, which was his only garment, drawn over

them inclosing his entire figure. He sat there like a sort of sculptured Egyptian cat or Peruvian mummy, moving nothing but his black eyes and looking absolutely non-human. This image and my fear entered into a species of combination with each other. *That shape am I*, I felt, potentially. Nothing that I possess can defend me against that fate, if the hour for it would strike for me as it struck for him. There was such a horror of him, and such a perception of my own merely momentary discrepancy from him, that it was as if something hitherto solid within my breast gave way entirely, and I became a mass of quivering fear. After this the universe was changed for me altogether. I awoke morning after morning with a horrible dread at the pit of my stomach, and with a sense of the insecurity of life that I never knew before, and that I have never felt since. It was like a revelation; and although the immediate feelings passed away, the experience has made me sympathetic with the morbid feelings of others ever since. It gradually faded, but for months I was unable to go out into the dark alone.

In general I dreaded to be left alone. I remember wondering how other people could

live, how I myself had ever lived, so uncon-
scious of that pit of insecurity beneath the
surface of life. My mother in particular, a very
cheerful person, seemed to me a perfect para-
dox in her unconsciousness of danger, which
you may well believe I was very careful not to
disturb by revelations of my own state of
mind. I have always thought that this experience of melancholia of mine had a religious
bearing.

I mean that the fear was so invasive and
powerful that if I had not clung to scripture-texts
like "The eternal God is my refuge," etc., "come
unto me, all ye that labor and are heavy-laden,"
etc. "I am the resurrection and the life," etc., I
think I should have grown really insane.[23]

It is not clear exactly how, or whether, this epi-
sode was connected with or grew out of Minny's
death. What is clearer, if not perfectly clear, is that
Minny's death set the terms in which William described the attack as an "experience" that "had a
religious bearing."

What happened next to William also may or
may not be directly connected with Minny's
death, but the spirit of resilience somehow came

upon him. On April 30, some seven weeks after Minny's death, he made an excited, upbeat entry in his journal:

> I think that yesterday was a crisis in my life. I finished the first part of Renouvier's 2nd Essay and saw no reason why his definition of free will—the sustaining of a thought because I choose to when I might have other thoughts— need be the definition of an illusion. At any rate, I will assume for the present—until next year—that it is no illusion. My first act of free will shall be to believe in free will.

The entry goes on to identify specific practical steps in this direction: "For the remainder of this year, I will abstain from mere speculation and con- templative *grubelei* [brooding, pondering] in which my nature takes most delight and voluntarily culti- vate the feeling of moral freedom, by reading books favorable to it, as well as by acting." James already understands the immense power of action— acting—as well as the power of habit. He goes on:

> Recollect that only when habits of order are formed can we advance to really interesting fields of action—and consequently accumulate grain

on grain of willful choice like a very miser—never forgetting that one link dropped undoes an infinite number . . . Today has furnished me the exceptionally passionate initiative which Bain posits as needful for the acquisition of habits. Not in maxims, not in *anschauungen* [perceptions, opinions] but in accumulated acts of thought lies salvation . . . Hitherto, when I have felt like taking a free initiative, like daring to act originally, without carefully waiting for contemplation of the external world to determine all for me, suicide seemed the most manly form to put my daring into. Now I will go a step further with my will, not only act with it, but believe as well; believe in my individual reality and creative power . . . My belief can't be optimistic, but I will posit it, life (the real, the good) in the self-governing resistance of the ego to the world. Life shall be built [on] doing and creating and suffering.[24]

This conclusion—that life, meaning what is real and what is good, exists in the "self-governing resistance of the ego to the world"—is the central insight, the pivotal moment of William James's life. It is much like Emerson's epiphany in the Jardin des Plantes, a moment of second birth—of something like conversion, from which comes a great deal of what he would achieve. The inclusion of the phrase "self-governing" links James's thought here to that of Alfred North Whitehead, who would say of reason that it is the "self-discipline of the originative element in history." Both statements emphasize the autonomy of the individual—*self*-governing, *self*-discipline—and both statements insist that self-generated change is possible.

This sentence about the self-governing resistance of the ego to the world is James's bedrock philosophical position, from which his central psychological convictions would follow. If we are free to choose one path over another, free to change some things (not all things), then it follows that we can change our attitude as well. And attitude, as the psychologist Mary Pipher has said, "may not be everything, but it is almost everything."[25]

18. The Self-Governing Resistance of the Ego to the World

James quickly began thinking about how to change his attitude. We can see it clearly in a letter he wrote on July 25, 1870, to his younger brother Robertson James:

I wish I could console you with religion
or philosophy. But I can't. Why you
should have been picked out to swell the
billions on whom fate has laid her rough
hand, who can say? But one thing is
certain, that through abridgement and
deprivation we learn of resources within
us, of whose existence we should else
have remained ignorant; of power to
resist pain, to rely on our own hearts
alone, to do without sympathy and
generally to keep our heads up under
circumstances where nothing but pure
courage will suffice. Death sits at the
heart of each one of us; some she takes
all at once, some she takes possession
of step by step, but sooner or later we
forfeit to her all that nature ever gave us.
Instead of skulking to escape her all our
days and being run down by her at last,
let us submit beforehand. We shall regret
less the loss of temporal happiness and
be able more undistractedly to think of
that alone which seems to belong to
us—to our wills—in life, namely the
keeping up of a true and courageous

spirit. Bitter though truth may be it seems
better to know it than not, and in that inner
solitary room of communion with his
own good will, there lies for every man
comfort.[26]

James wrote this letter to Robertson a little
more than four months after Minny Temple died.
We cannot, of course, say that her death *caused*
the dramatic emergence of William James's central insight ("the self-governing resistance of the
ego to the world"), but only that the insight arrived in the wake of Minny's death. The *reason* for
the resilience shown here is not clear. What is
clear is that William either already had or quickly
acquired the resilience needed to get out of the
long, depressed state of mind that culminated in
Minny's death and in William's strange vision of
the green-skinned idiot in the asylum. James had
the resilience when he needed it most.

———

William James went on to a long and productive
career in psychology and philosophy, and it is
striking how some of his most important and

most influential ideas have to do with what we
might call strategies for encouraging resilience. In
an 1884 essay "What is an emotion," James out-
lines an approach, later called cognitive behavioral therapy, in which a person can change his
thinking—change his attitude—and in turn help
change behavior. The central paragraph is also
the first version of what would become known as
the James-Lange theory of emotion, which is
that the emotion follows an action, rather than
having an action follow from an emotion. James's
1884 description of the process was reproduced
almost word for word in his 1890 *Principles of
Psychology*:

Everyone knows how panic is increased by
flight, and how the giving way to the symptoms
of grief or anger increases those passions themselves. Each fit of sobbing makes the sorrow
more acute, and calls forth another fit stronger
still, until at last repose only ensues with lassi-
tude and with the apparent exhaustion of the
machinery. In rage it is notorious how we
"work ourselves up" to a climax by repeated
outbreaks of expression. Refuse to express a
passion and it dies. Count ten before venting

your anger, and its occasion seems ridiculous. Whistling to keep up courage is no mere figure of speech. On the other hand, sit all day in a moping posture, sigh, and reply to everything with a dismal voice, and your melancholy lingers. There is no more valuable precept in moral education than this, as all who have experience know. If we wish to conquer undesirable emotional tendencies in ourselves, we must assiduously, and in the first instance cold-bloodedly, go through the *outward movements* of those contrary dispositions which we prefer to cultivate. The reward of persistency will infallibly come, in the fading out of the sullenness or depression and the advent of real cheerfulness and kindliness in their stead. Smooth the brow, brighten the eye, contract the dorsal rather than the ventral aspect of the frame, and speak in a major key, pass the genial compliment, and your heart must be frigid indeed if it do not gradually thaw![27]

We can, if we need to, change our minds and our behaviors. Experts disagree about whether we must first change our mental attitude to produce practical physical change or, more radically, whether if we can change our behavior, the mind will follow suit, as in "refuse to express a passion and it dies." Either way can produce the kind of change that favors and empowers resilience.

Minny Temple had a major impact on several lives. Her death marks the point at which William James began his climb out of depression and sickness. John Gray kept her letters all his life. Henry James came to write, in the last chapter of *Notes of a Son and Brother*, a memorial tribute of novella length about Minny. And Alice James, William's wife, wrote her brother-in-law on March 14, 1914, four years after William had died: "You may not understand in the least how I feel, but it almost seems to me as if I had all that she deserved. Were you ever haunted by a 'vicarious Atonement' feeling? That someone else was going without that you might be blessed?"[28]

Postscript

Resilience is not in general quirky or unusual, nor is it a resource available only to those of iron will who can alter their views or transcend their feelings. Resilience is built into us and into things. Of the persons treated in this book, Emerson had the most profound and nuanced understanding of the real nature of resilience, and of the extent to which we, and all of nature, are caught up in it. Emerson called the process "compensation." That is the title of the third essay in his *Essays First Series* (1841). The subject had fascinated him since childhood, he tells us, and he began to seriously work up the subject for a series of lectures he gave in 1837. In 1839, the year his daughter Ellen was born, he was still working on it. Coming right after "History" and "Self-Reliance," "Compensation" remains a crucial leg of Emerson's thought, and the best single statement of how the resilience we sometimes feel in ourselves is in truth a universal law or force, discernable anywhere one looks. Resilience is part of the nature of things.

In the last paragraph of "Compensation," Emerson acknowledges that everything has two sides and says we are free to choose one of those sides:

> And yet the compensations of calamity are made apparent to the understanding also, after long intervals of time. A fever, a mutilation, a cruel disappointment, a loss of wealth, a loss of friends, seem at the moment unpaid loss, and unpayable. But the sure years reveal the deep remedial force that underlies all facts. The death of a dear friend, wife, brother, lover, which seemed nothing but privation, somewhat later assumes the aspect of a guide or genius; for it commonly operates revolutions in our way of life, terminates an epoch of infancy or of youth which was waiting to be closed, breaks up a wonted occupation, or a household, or style of living, and allows the formation of new ones more friendly to the growth of character.

We may pause to note that Emerson himself experienced every single loss here enumerated. His account of recovery is not just happy talk or routine uplift or marketable optimism. A final example, from the last paragraph of the essay "Montaigne" from Emerson's 1850 book *Representative Men*, shows how deeply Emerson could feel this recovery:

> The lesson of life is practically to generalize; to believe what the years and the centuries say against the hours; to resist the usurpation of particulars; to penetrate to their catholic sense. Things seem to say one thing and say the reverse. The appearance is immoral, the result is moral. Things seem to tend downward, to justify despondency, to promote rogues, to defeat the just; and by knaves as by martyrs the just cause is carried forward. Although knaves win in every political struggle, although society seems to be delivered over from the hands of one set of criminals into the hands of another set of criminals, as fast as the government is changed, and the march of civilization is a train of felonies, yet, general ends are somehow answered.

There is a lot of resilience hidden in that word "somehow."

NOTES

Abbreviations

JMN   *Journals and Miscellaneous Notebooks of Ralph Waldo Emerson* (Cambridge, MA: Harvard University Press, 1960–1982)

PJ   *The Writings of Henry D. Thoreau: Journal* (Princeton, NJ: Princeton University Press, 1982–)

PJ Corr   *The Correspondence of Henry D. Thoreau* (Princeton, NJ: Princeton University Press, 2013–)

Preface

1. There are now many clinical studies of resilience. See, for example, Steven M. Southwick and Dennis S. Charney, *Resilience: The Science of Mastering Life's Greatest Challenges*, 2nd ed. (Cambridge: Cambridge University Press, 2018).

2. An excellent recent example of documentary biography is Jeffrey S. Cramer's *Solid Seasons* (Berkeley, CA: Counterpoint Press, 2019), which tells the story of the connection between Emerson and Thoreau mainly through their own words.

Part I. Emerson

1. Emerson got the most striking sentence of this declaration from a story in Herodotus, in which a Spartan soldier is warned that the oncoming Persian archers will blot out the sun with their arrows and the soldier replies that they will fight better in the shade.

2. JMN 3:226, entry dated February 13, 1831.

3. Ellen Louisa (Emerson) Tucker, *One First Love: The Letters of Ellen Louisa Tucker to Ralph Waldo Emerson*, edited by Edith W. Gregg (Cambridge, MA: Harvard University Press, 1962), pp. 145–168.

4. The first line of this poem is "And when I am entombed in my place." It appears in *The Complete Works of Ralph Waldo Emerson: Poems* [Vol. 9], edited by Edward Waldo Emerson (Boston: Houghton Mifflin, 1903–1904), p. 395, and is titled "Written in Naples," dated 1833.

5. JMN 3:313.

6. *The Complete Works of Ralph Waldo Emerson: English Traits* [Vol. 5], edited by Edward Waldo Emerson (Boston: Houghton Mifflin, 1903–1904), *English Traits*, p. 189.

7. JMN 4:27.

8. Still the best formulation of this is Cato's *rem tene, verba sequntur* (Hold fast to things; words will follow). See JMN 4:106.

9. JMN 4:72.

10. JMN 4:199–200.

11. JMN 4:200.

12. *Edinburgh Review*, July 1832.

13. JMN 4:83.

14. Ibid.

15. *The Complete Works of Ralph Waldo Emerson: English Traits* [Vol. 5], edited by Edward Waldo Emerson (Boston: Houghton Mifflin, 1903–1904), *English Traits*, p. 189.

16. Emerson, "The Uses of Natural History," quoted in Robert D. Richardson, *Emerson: The Mind on Fire* (Berkeley: University of California Press, 1995), p. 154.

17. Richardson, *Emerson: The Mind on Fire*, p. 155.

18. *The Early Lectures of Ralph Waldo Emerson*, Vol. 1, edited by Stephen E. Whicher and Robert E. Spiller (Cambridge, MA: Harvard University Press, 1959), p. 26.

Part II. Thoreau

1. PJ 1:3534. The present chapter is essentially a biographer's unpacking of the startling and persuasive insights of Branka Arsic's *Bird Relics: Grief and Vitalism in Thoreau* (Cambridge, MA: Harvard University Press, 2016) and a reworking of those insights in a more narrative form. Arsic's work may have minor flaws—she uses the word imagination as though it meant seeing things that aren't there—but the brilliance and drive of her insights into how Thoreau's mind worked are undeniable and of major importance.

2. JMN 8:205, January 27, 1842.

3. The final entry in Thoreau's journal is, "After a violent easterly storm in the night, which clears up at noon (November 3, 1861) I notice that the surface of the railroad causeway, composed of gravel, is singularly marked, as if stratified like some slate rocks, on their edges, so that I can tell, within a fraction of a degree from what quarter the rain came. These lines, as it were of stratification, are perfectly parallel, and straight as a ruler, diagonally across the flat surface of the causeway for its whole length. Behind each little pebble, as a protecting boulder, an eighth or a tenth of an inch in diameter, extends northwest a ridge of sand an inch or more, which it has protected from being washed away, while the heavy drops driven almost horizontally have washed out a furrow on each side, and on all sides are these ridges, half an inch apart and perfectly parallel.

"All this is perfectly distinct to an observant eye, and yet could easily pass unnoticed by most. Thus each wind is self-registering."

4. PJ 1:369.

5. PJ 1:365.

6. PJ Corr 1:102.

7. Ibid.

8. PJ 1:368.

9. PJ Corr 1:104.

10. PJ Corr 1:104–105.

11. PJ 1:372.

12. PJ 1:372–373.

13. PJ 1:374.

14. PJ Corr 1:108.

15. PJ 1:375.

16. PJ 1:379.

17. Thoreau, Journal 1906, Dover reprint Vol. 1, p. 340. PJ 1:383. The phrase "my friend is my real brother" is included in the 1906 edition of *The Journal of Henry D. Thoreau*, edited by Bradford Torrey and Francis H. Allen, which was reprinted by Dover Publications in 1962. The sentence does not appear in the Princeton edition of the journal. There are several more penciled-in phrases and sentences visible on a photocopy of this one manuscript page, which I received from Beth Witherell. The original is in the Morgan Library (New York) in the volumes accessioned as MA 1302:6. The additional penciled lines are very difficult to discern, and no reconstruction has appeared in any edition of the journal.

18. PJ 1:384.

19. Emerson mentions the reports in his journal, and is reading the Colman volume, which he did not send to Thoreau, according to a journal entry of April 13, 1842. JMN 8:234.

20. JMN 8:232.

21. H. D. Thoreau, *Excursions*, edited by J. J. Moldenhauer (Princeton, NJ: Princeton University Press, 2007), p. 8.

22. Ibid., pp. 9–10.

23. Ibid., p. 28.

24. "Spring," *Walden*, edited by J. Lyndon Shanley (Princeton, NJ: Princeton University Press, 2004), p. 318.

Part III. William James

1. William James's Diary is archived at Harvard University. The call number for the years 1868–1873 is bMS Am 1092.9 (4550). This entry is dated July 22, 1868.

2. Letter dated January 15, 1870, printed in *The Correspondence of William James*, Vol. 4 (Charlottesville: University of Virginia Press, 1992), p. 401.

3. William James Diary entry for March 22, 1870, Harvard Manuscript bMS Am 1092.9 (4550).

4. Henry James, *Notes of a Son and Brother* (New York: Charles Scribner's Sons, 1914), p. 429.

5. Letter to J. C. Gray, Harvard Manuscript HU bMS Am 1092.12 folder 2.

6. Henry James, *Notes of a Son and Brother*, p. 430.

7. Ibid., chapter 13.

8. *Correspondence of William James*, Vol. 1, p. 153.

9. Ibid.

10. Ibid., p. 154.

11. Ibid.

12. Ibid.

13. By far the best account of Minny Temple and her importance for Henry James is Lyndall Gordon, *The Private Life of Henry James* (London: Chatto and Windus, 1998).

14. Henry James, *The Ambassadors* (New York: Harper & Brothers, 1903), Part Fifth, II.

15. Henry James, *Notes of a Son and Brother*, p. 479.

16. Ibid.

17. Letter to Katherine Temple Emmet, November 1861, in *Correspondence of William James*, Vol. 4, p. 48.

18. *Correspondence of William James*, Vol. 1, p. 124.

19. Harvard Manuscript bMS Am 1092.12 (folder 3).

20. Ibid. (folder 2).

21. Harvard Manuscript bMS Am 1092.9 (4550).

22. *Correspondence of William James*, Vol. 4, pp. 401–403.

23. William wrote this in his diary some time in April 1870. The original has not survived. The text here is from William James, *The Varieties of Religious Experience* (Cambridge, MA: Harvard University Press, 1985), pp. 134–135, identified as his own experience in a footnote therein.

24. William James Diary, April 30, 1870.

25. Mary Pipher, "The Joy of Being a Woman in Her 70s," *New York Times*, January 12, 2019.

26. *Correspondence of William James*, Vol. 4, p. 409.

27. William James, *The Principles of Psychology* (Cambridge, MA: Harvard University Press, 1981), Vol. 2, ch. 25, pp. 1077–1078.

28. Lyndall Gordon, *The Private Life of Henry James*, p. 354.

INDEX

Agassiz, Louis, 77

Alcott, Louisa May, 34, 43

The Ambassadors (Henry James), 74–75

Audubon, John James, 29

Bain, Alexander, 89

Bartlett, Josiah, 30, 33

Bate, Walter Jackson, xi

Bell, Charles, 31

Brown, Lucy Jackson, 39–41

Bryden, William, 32–33

The Burden of the Past (Bate), xi

Carlyle, Jane (Welsh), 15, 17

Carlyle, Thomas, 7, 10, 15–20, 24

Chandogya, 68

Chaucer, Geoffrey, 30, 38

cognitive behavioral therapy, 92–93

Coleridge, Samuel Taylor, 15

Colman, Henry, 52

"Compensation" (Emerson), 52, 96–97

Corn Law Rhymes (Elliott), 16–17

Daisy Miller (Henry James), 74

Darwin, Charles, 77

Dewey, Chester, 53

Dial, 52, 54, 63

Dickens, Charles, 33

documentary biography, x, xix

Edinburgh Review, 18

Eichhorn, Johann Gottfried, 5

Elliott, Ebenezer, 16–17

Ellis (ship captain), 11

Emerson, Charles (brother), 12–13, 25

Emerson, Ellen (daughter), 96

Emerson, Ellen Tucker (wife): as aspiring poet, 4; death of, 1–3, 62

Emerson, Lydia (Lidian) Jackson (wife), 24, 32, 33
Emerson, Mary Moody (aunt), 24
Emerson, Ralph Waldo, 1, 32, 33; Carlyle's friendship with, 15–20, 24; deceased family members of, xii; as *Dial* editor, 52–53; European journey of, 11–20; formal Christianity renounced by, 7–11, 25, 62; on genius, xiii; independent thought professed by, 7; in Jardin des Plantes, 13, 14, 21–22, 24, 27, 28, 89; Jesus slighted by, 24–25; language interests of, 18, 23; on Lord's Supper, 8–9, 63; as minister, 4–5, 7; "miserable apathy" of, 2, 3; nature likened to language by, 23–24, 36; on oral law, 19; resilience understood by, 96–97; scientific interests of, 5–7, 13–15, 21–22; self-reliance viewed by, xvii–xviii; son's death and, 33–34; Thoreau's friendship with, 35, 36, 50, 61; on wife's death, 2–3
Emerson, Waldo (son), 25, 33, 38–42, 72

Emerson, William (brother), 5, 33
English Traits (Emerson), 20
Essays, First Series (Emerson), 52, 96

Fichte, Johann Gottlieb, 18
Fourth Report on the Agriculture of Massachusetts (Colman), 52–53
Fuller, Margaret, 52
The Function of Reason (Whitehead), 46

Gay-Lussac, Joseph-Louis, 13
German Higher Criticism, 5
Gray, John, 73, 78, 79, 95

Herschel, John, 6
Hinduism, 70
"History" (Emerson), 52, 96
Holmes, Oliver Wendell, Jr., 73

James, Alice, 95
James, Catherine, 69
James, Henry, 36, 68; Minny Temple recalled by, 69–74, 76
James, Henry, Sr., 36, 69, 83
James, Robertson, 90–92
James, William, 32, 43, 65, 73; cousin's death and, 66–68;

emotional troubles of,
85–87, 92, 94–95; on free
will, 88–89; Minny Temple
recalled by, 76–78; Minny
Temple's closeness to,
78–79, 84–85; truth as
process viewed by, xvii
James-Lange theory of
emotion, 93
Jasper (ship), 11–12
John the Apostle, Saint, 9

Keats, John, 42

Laplace, Pierre Simon, 5
Luke, the Apostle, Saint, 9

Mark, the Apostle, Saint, 9
materialism, 19
Matthew, the Apostle, Saint, 9
Mechanism of the Heavens
(Somerville), 5
Mill, John Stuart, 17
"Montaigne" (Emerson), 98

"Natural History of Intellect"
(Emerson), 27
"Natural History of Massachusetts" (Thoreau), 54–58,
60, 61–63
Nature (Emerson), 10, 22, 23,
25–27, 43, 52

negative capability, 42, 58
Notes of a Son and Brother
(Henry James), 69,
75, 95

Oegger, Guillaume, 35–36

Peabody, Elizabeth, 35
Pipher, Mary, 90
"The Poet" (Emerson), xiii
Portrait of a Lady (Henry
James), 74
*Preliminary Discourse on the
Study of Natural Philosophy*
(Herschel), 6
Principles of Psychology
(William James), 93–94

Renouvier, Charles, 88
Representative Men (Emerson),
98
resilience, xviii, 61, 62, 64,
87–88, 92, 96–98
Richardson, John, xiv

Schelling, Friedrich Wilhelm
Joseph von, 18
self-reliance, xvii–xviii
"Self-Reliance" (Emerson),
52, 96
Somerville, Mary, 5
Swedenborg, Emanuel, 36

Temple, Katherine, 76

Temple, Minny, 66–69; death of, 72, 74–75, 84, 94; Henry James's recollections of, 69–74, 76; religious struggle of, 78, 80–84; William James's closeness to, 78–79, 84–85

Tetanus Following Gunshot Wounds (Bell), 31

Thenard, Louis-Jacques, 13

Thoreau: A Life of the Mind (Richardson), xi

Thoreau, Henry David, xvii; brother's death and, 30–32; creativity vs. entropy viewed by, 49; on death, 43–48, 60–61; ecocentric vision of, 57–58, 61–62; Emerson's friendship with, 35, 36, 50, 61; on friendship, 50–52, 60; on grief, 40–41; health emphasized by, 55–56; journal amended by, 39; journal writing resumed by, 34–35; on sounds of nature, 37, 57; structural weaknesses in writing of, 56–57; on Waldo's death, 43, 72; writings for the *Dial* by, 52–56

Thoreau, John (brother), xiv, 30–32, 38, 39–42, 54

transcendentalism, 18

The True Messiah (Oegger), 35

Unitarianism, 7, 15, 19, 27, 81

"The Uses of Natural History" (Emerson), 21–23, 25, 26, 62

utilitarianism, 19

Varieties of Religious Experience (William James), 85

Walden (Thoreau), 46–47, 58–59, 61–62

Walls, Laura, 54

Welsh (Carlyle), Jane, 15, 17

"What is an emotion" (William James), 92–93

Whitehead, Alfred North, 46, 90

Williams, Isaiah, 48

The Will to Believe (William James), 65

The Wings of the Dove (Henry James), 74

Wordsworth, William, 17